D0521083

ABOUT THE PUBLISHER

The New York Inst

NYIF offers practical, appli
range of formats and topics

* *Classroom training:* even
* *Seminars and conferences:*
  tory, intermediate-, and
* *Customized training:* nee
  your site or ours; in New
  States, anywhere in the
* *Independent study:* self-
  or advanced
* *Exam preparation:* NASI
  24, 27, 63); C.F.A.; state

Subjects of books and trai
* Account Executive Trair
* Brokerage Operations
* Currency Trading
* Futures Trading
* International Corporate
* Investment Analysis

When Wall Street professior

For further information,
cify your areas of interest
rams, independent-study
books—so that we can re

New York I
2 Broadway
New York, I
212 / 859-5(
FAX: 212 /

"Where Wal

TECHNICAL
ANALYSIS
A Personal Seminar

Preface

Technical analysis is a time-proven method of forecasting the prices of stocks, futures contracts, indexes, or any kind of financial instrument. You can apply it to any investment or trading vehicle because you focus exclusively on price action, not on the underlying reasons for the movement of prices up, down, or sideways. The basic premise is that history repeats itself. Specifically, given a set of conditions, the participants in a market are going to react, in the aggregate, pretty much the same way all the time. The collective activities of participants show up on the technician's charts as patterns—patterns that repeat themselves. If you record the price movements of an instrument or market, eventually these patterns emerge, along with buy and sell signals. In many cases, you can even calculate the minimum extent of a trend, thereby knowing when to get into the market and when to get out.

Despite the effectiveness of technical analysis, its techniques are simple and easy to learn. The real test of a successful technical analyst, however, is the seasoned individual judgment that comes with experience. This *Personal Seminar* will acquaint you with the basics of technical analysis, thereby enabling you to begin charting and start gaining that experience right away. Without knowing the basics, the experience gained from transactions can be costly.

Technical Analysis: A Personal Seminar:

- Explains the underlying assumptions of this method.
- Shows you how to construct the two basic types of charts.
- Describes the fundamental concepts of price action.
- Then challenges you to work with the major patterns.

Throughout the book, frequent examples enable you to test your knowledge in hands-on, how-to exercises.

All you need to get started, besides this *Seminar*, is a pad of graph paper with a quarter-inch grid. (You might also want to get a pad with eighth-inch grid paper, but only if you are interested in doing a lot of what is known as "point and figure" charting. At the outset, quarter-inch paper will meet your needs.)

Note: Throughout most of the *Seminar*, fictitious stock is used in the examples. If your aim is to trade futures, options, indexes, or any other instrument, all the information and exercises apply just as well. In addition, wherever appropriate, additional comments are added to cover futures trading, an area that varies the most from all others.

TECHNICAL ANALYSIS

A Personal Seminar

1

Introduction to Technical Analysis

Who can predict stock price levels? Can the past be used to forecast turns in the market? Anticipating future peaks and troughs—buying low and selling high—is the cardinal principle of investing. Yet, like so many maxims, it is easy to grasp but typically impossible to execute. Each investor or trader seems to have his or her own individual method. Yet all the approaches tend to fall into one or the other of two categories of analysis: fundamental or technical.

Fundamental analysts attempt to evaluate a company's prospects for growth and profitability in light of the outlook for the economy, the firm's industry, and the company itself. Although there is no universally accepted approach, a three-phase process is widely accepted: First, the overall economic environment, both domestic and international, is assessed for elements that either favor or discourage the success of the company in question. Second, the industry is scrutinized for its effects on the company (or futures contract); also, the company's financial ratios and other performance indicators are compared to industry standards. Finally, the company itself is evaluated for its ability to perform within the economic and industry setting. In futures trading, the contract is studied with the purpose of determining price reactions to relevant conditions—such as the effect of a drought on corn prices or an OPEC decision on oil. On the basis of all this research, fundamentalists then project the future price level of the stock or futures contract.

Adherents to the fundamentalist method thus attempt to to discern cause-and-effect relationships between a security and its price. They amass information on interest rates, the trade and budget deficits, the consumer price index, commodity scarcities, and other economic influences. They collect data on the relevant industry and how it is likely to fare in times to come. They pore over a company's financial statements, auditor's reports, dividend history, profit and loss statements, and balance sheets. They learn as much as they can about the company's management, its plant capacity, and other particulars. They compare the company against others in the same business, its competitors, and against industry standards. In futures, they put together as many facts as they can about a commodity's "environment," whether that environment is a mine worker's strike in South Africa or the Fed's influence on interest rates.

Having done all this research and having formulated their conclusions, fundamentalists attempt to forecast the future price of the company's stocks (or bonds). If they foresee a rise in price, they may buy the instrument—that is, "go long." In anticipation of a decline, they may either sell the instrument or sell it short. In brief, fundamental analysts base their investment activities on the causes of price movement.

Technical analysts do not attempt to explain why prices move as they do. Their aim is to measure the supply an demand for a security or other financial vehicle so as to predict future price levels and movements. They attempt to detect patterns in market action that they can identify as having happened often enough in the past to be reliable as an indicator of future price levels. For example, if the price of a stock moves up, then down, back up higher still, and down again, it is possible that a pattern could be forming known as a "head and shoulders." It looks like this (the solid lines A-E represent the activity to date, and the dashed lines E-G show the expected movement):

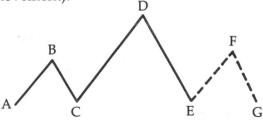

If the pattern is indeed a head and shoulders, then technical analysts know that the market will rebound (E to F). They will buy at the last downturn (E) and wait for the market to rise again to the next "shoulder" (F), where they can sell off and possibly buy again at the next low (G).

Thus technical analysts, or "chartists" as they are also called, do not try to explain why prices move as they do. Their only concern is that prices move in predictable patterns. Technical analysis is the study of the market action itself. The intrinsic value of the stock—or bond or option or futures contract or index—is irrelevant.

To many people, especially the curious ones, not knowing why something happens seems unscienticific. Why wouldn't chartists want and need to know the causes of market action?

The Assumptions of Technical Analysis

To answer that question, you must understand the primary assumptions of technical analysis:

- Market action discounts everything.
- Prices move in trends.
- History repeats itself.

Market Action

The working principle is that any influence on the market is already reflected in current price levels. In its simplest form, this assumption means that price action reflects shifts in the relative degrees of supply and/or demand. If supply exceeds demand, prices decline; if demand outweighs supply, prices rise.

This simple assumption is carried forward to apply to any condition that would cause prices to move: The market is said to "discount" all influences on it. Whatever causes stock prices to go up or down—changing economic conditions, rumors of war, fluctuating interest rates, news of a merger, and so on—is already reflected in the prices of current trades. By the time you figure out the reasons for those prices, the market has passed you by. Further, trying to forecast prices by analyzing all the influences on a market is futile; there are just too many for anyone to properly analyze them, do the number crunching, come up with the winning investment strategy, and execute it in time to make a profit.

Knowing the reasons for price movement is therefore helpful to chartists but not essential to their success.

Note: In futures trading, supply and demand for futures contracts can differ from supply and demand for the underlying commodity or instrument. For example, if there is a large crop of corn (the commodity), demand may be low, and prices tend to fall. Demand for corn futures contracts, however, may still be high among traders attempting to capitalize on the dropping prices of corn.

Price Trends

Technicians presume that a price continues to move in a given direction until something occurs to change its direction. A price trend does not reverse itself; only outside influences can do that. A corollary of this assumption is that price trends are more likely to continue than they are to change direction. This principle is essential to forecasting on the basis of charting.

History Repeats Itself

History repeats itself, technicians maintain, because people "repeat" themselves. Human psychology being what it is, investors and traders tend to react the same way to a set of market conditions every time they occur. These human reactions become buy and sell transactions in the marketplace, all of which chartists record as patterns that are to a great degree predictable. Given the huge numbers of participants in most markets, the probability is very high that the overall pattern of buying and selling will be same from one occasion to the next—that the resultant pattern on the technician's chart will be the same also.

Technical Versus Fundamental Analysis

These two schools of thought seem so much at odds that it would seem inevitable that a great deal of debate goes on between them. And indeed one does. Certain adherents of both schools simply refuse to admit the validity of the opposing theory. We've already heard the argument for technical analysis. Staunch fundamentalists, on the other hand, argue back with the "random walk theory," which holds that price movements occur without pattern. This theory is based on the "efficient market hypothesis," which is the assumption that the market is "efficient" in discounting all the influences on it. (Yes, this sounds very much like the basis of the argument for the futility of the fundamental approach.) The reasoning is that, with so many and diverse conditions impacting on the market, it is impossible for any discernible pattern to occur consistently. The mix of influences is too varied and too shifting to be relied on for repetition. Hence the random walk theory concludes that the only sensible strategy is to buy and hold, not to try to beat the market.

Given the head-on opposition between the two approaches, an analyst is generally either a technician or a fundamentalist, hardly ever both. Yet using both methods only makes sense. Many investors adopt a fundamental approach to select their investments and then use charts to pick the times to get into and out of the market. Others follow the market on their charts and then take fundamentalist measures to choose particular stocks or contracts.

Despite the widespread agreement that a combined approach makes sense, the debate rages on, and it is likely to continue for many years to come. Suffice it to say that the technical approach can be of great assistance to anyone seeking to enhance returns through better timing. And that goes even if you are a fundamentalist at heart. Most chartists will insist, despite your leanings, that the appearance of randomness diminishes as you learn the technical approach.

The Dow Theory

No introduction to technical analysis is complete without an explanation of the Dow Theory.

Charles H. Dow never published the "theory" he founded. Rather, it grew out of his work with stock market averages, which were mathematical averages of a carefully selected "basket" of stocks, the now famous Dow Jones Averages. He left it to others to compile the "theory" from his many scattered writings about the averages—a handful of tenets that act as the underpinning of modern technical analysis. Some of them will be familiar to you:

1. The averages discount everything except acts of God. If this sounds a lot like one of the basic principles of technical analysis, you're right.

2. There are three types of trends:

- The major (or primary) trends last for more than a year and often for many years.
- Secondary (or intermediate) corrections may endure for several weeks to several months. They are also called "corrections" because they are regarded as interruptions in the major trend. They may retrace from one-third to two-thirds of a price trend but only temporarily. Ultimately the long-term trend is reasserted.
- Minor corrections last from a week to several weeks, and there may be two or three of them within an intermediate type of trend.

3. The major trends go through three phases.

- During the "accumulation" stage, when price levels are relatively low, informed investors are buying, or "accumulating" positions.
- As more buyers—and perhaps less astute ones—join in buying, prices advance rapidly; this is the second phase, the so-called "bull market model." Sooner or later, there is a buying climax, in which the "dogs and cats" (lower quality stocks) are caught up in the buying enthusiasm with the high-quality securities. By this time the market has likely been going up for years.
- Suddenly prices seem untenably high, the market generally overpriced. When first the sophisticated investors and then other less adroit holders start to sell off in greater and greater numbers, the third phase, called the "bear market" or "distribution" stage, has begun. The "longs" are "distributing" their holdings to those who are willing to buy.

4. The averages must confirm each other. Although Dow was referring to the Rail and Industrial averages, he was touching on the much broader and more significant principles of confirmation and divergence. No one indicator in technical analysis can be regarded as the one-and-only signal; indicators must confirm each for the buy or sell signal to be considered valid.

5. Volume must confirm the trend. Over time, Dow came to realize that movements in the direction of the major trend almost always were accompanied by heavy or increasing volume. Upward movements could be considered part of a trend if heavy volume occurred simultaneously; conversely, great volume on down-swings indicated a bear market tendency.

6. Trends will continue until there is a definite signal of a reversal. Again, stating this principle is easier than putting into play. When is a contrary price movement a temporary correction and when is it the first leg of a major reversal? This is perhaps the hardest question to answer for any trend-follower—and one we will address later in the book.

As you can see, the Dow Theory acts as the theoretical foundation for technical analysis.

Nevertheless, the theory has been subject to criticisms, perhaps the most relevant of which is that the Dow Theory does not allow the intermediate trader to take advantage of price movements. For the most part, that's true. On average about 20% to 25% of a movement is complete before the trend-watcher notices the signal. By then it may be too late to capitalize on the price action. On the other hand, the Dow Theory was never intended to benefit the short-term or intermediate trader. It was rather meant to serve the interests of the long-term investor. Nevertheless some traders have worked out methods by which they can capture a fair share of intermediate-term movements.

Another criticism has been that you can't trade the averages. Of course, now you can by means of the options and futures contracts on averages and indexes.

Certainly the Dow Theory is not infallible. No theory, no system, no approach is. So it is with technical analysis. As we proceed through the upcoming chapters, you will see how these techniques are applied, how the results are interpreted, and how to act on your conclusions. Through it all, remember that technical analysis is a skill that, like any skill, must be practiced. This book can show you how to construct charts, how to read them, how to recognize the classic buy and sell signals. But no system will give you one-hundred-percent certain signals. Ultimately the decision to buy or sell is yours. Technical analysis, like any other analytical method, can only help you to make higher-quality decisions.

2
Charts

Technical analysts are not, strictly speaking, chartists. A chartist is someone who prepares the graph-like records of price movement. An analyst, on the other hand, may prepare charts but is more likely someone who specializes in the analysis of the charts themselves. This distinction is reflected in the fact that most analysts make use of chart services, some of which are in printed form but most of which are offered on electronic media. There are numerous charts services for you to take advantage of, and the most up-to-date and useful are the ones that come in the form of a data base. A relatively inexpensive desktop personal computer enables you to access these services.

Nevertheless, to be able to read and interpret a chart, you should know how one is constructed. Also, it is possible that the type of chart you need is not available on any service, and you will need to prepare your own.

Charts can take many forms. They can reflect monthly, weekly, daily, and even intraday data. They can include just price movement or a large number of other types of indicators, such as volume, open interest, oscillators, ratios, short interest, and so on. The scale they use can be arithmetic or logarithmic.

Of the countless types of charts possible, we will focus on what is known as the "daily bar chart," plotted on an arithmetic scale. This chart is the most widely used (hourly, or intraday, charts are used primarily by professional traders). And, if you understand how a daily bar chart works, you can create and interpret most other types of charts.

Types of Charts

The two basic types of charts are:

• Bar (see Figure 2-1).
• Point and figure (P&F, see Figure 2-2).

FIGURE 2-1   A typical bar chart.

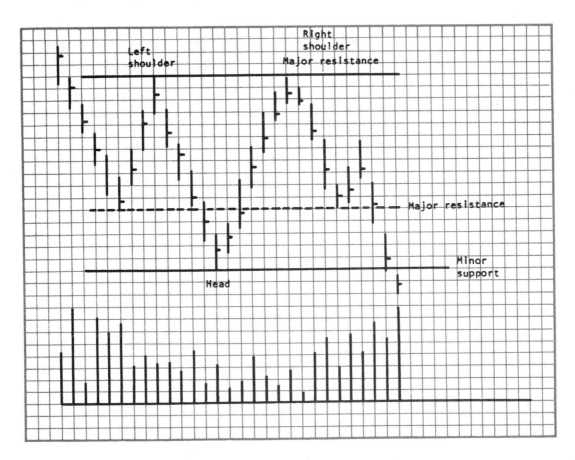

FIGURE 2-2   A typical point and figure (P&F) chart.

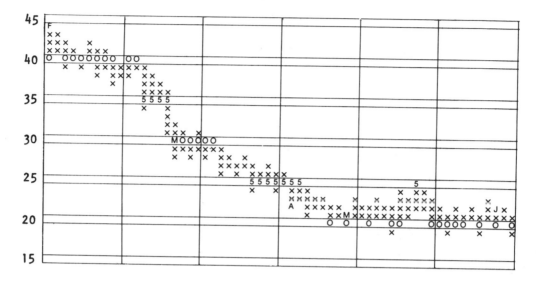

Of the two, the bar chart is capable of containing more information. Volume, for example, can be included at the foot of the chart, and an oscillator line (explained in Chapter 3) included between the volume and the price data. In addition, the bar chart reflects time periods, whereas point and figure charts do not: On a bar chart, there is an entry for every day (week, hour, or other unit of time), even if a price remains unchanged. On a P&F chart, if there is no price change, there is no entry; if a thinly traded stock trades only once a week, then a whole week's worth of trading on the P&F chart will consist of one entry. Consequently, almost all electronic chart services appear in the form of bar charts.

Almost all services also use an arithmetic, as opposed to a logarithmic, scale. Notice, in Figure 2-3, the equal spacing between the tic marks on the arithmetic scale, compared with the unequal spacing on the logarithmic scale. As you can see, the values assigned to the tic marks on both scales are the same, but watch what happens. If a stock rises from $5 to $10, that's a 100% increase. But a rise from $50 to $55 is only a 10% increase. On an arithmetic scale, both price rises are reflected with the same length on the axis; on the log scale, the greater percentage increase occupies more of the vertical scale. The visual depiction of the percentage increase is thus better on the logarithmic than on the arithmetic scale.

FIGURE 2-3   Arithmetic and logarithmic scales.

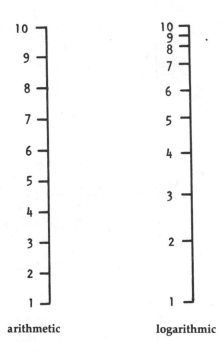

arithmetic   logarithmic

Despite this fact, arithmetic scales are what you see on commercial chart services, probably because they are what people are used to seeing. By analogy, take a baseball player's batting average early in the season. On opening day, a batter gets up three times: He strikes out and then gets two hits. His batting average is .000 after the first time at bat, .500 after the first hit (he's one for two), and .667 by the end of the game (two for three). Between the first and second hits, the batting average jumped 33% from .500 to .667—with one hit! As the season wears on, however, and the number of times at bat increases, each hit will have less and less effect on the batting average. Toward the end of the season, a hit will nudge the batting average only a fraction of a point. Why, then, aren't batting averages scaled logarithmically?

The answer is—for the same reason that most bar charts are not: The value added is negligible. While you might want to prepare your own charts on log scale graph paper, you will be hard pressed to find a service that offers data in this format.

So we will spend most of our time learning and using daily bar charts on an arithmetic scale.

Bar Charts

Paper Needed

For bar charts the best kind of graph paper has a grid of four squares to an inch for stocks trading under $30 and eight squares to an inch for stocks over $30. The simple reason is that ¼" squares, although easy to use, require much larger, difficult-to-handle sheets for higher-priced securities. If price movement runs off the edge of the original sheet and you want a continuous chart, simple tape other sheets to the top, bottom, or edges of first sheet. Be sure to overlap the sheets slightly and to align the grids very precisely.

Also desirable for daily bar charting is a heavy line on every fifth grid. This marks the beginning of a new week. If your graph paper does not have this feature, you can darken the fifth lines with a pen, or simply mark them with calendar dates or some other weekly indicator.

Construction

When starting a chart, lay out the sheet of paper so that the 11′ sides are vertical. Insert the name of the stock, the bond, futures contract, or market at the top left corner of the sheet, followed by the year.

Then you have to set up three scales:

- Time scale (below the horizontal axis).
- Volume scale (along the bottom of the vertical axis).
- Price movement scale (along the top of the vertical axis).

The volume and price movement scales are usually on the left, although some chartists also repeat the scale on the right. See Figure 2-4, which contains a chart for ABC stock.

Time Scale

Select a horizontal grid line at least two rows of boxes from the bottom of the graph paper, come in about four or five boxes from the left edge of the graph paper, and darken the horizontal line all

FIGURE 2-4   The completed ABC bar chart.

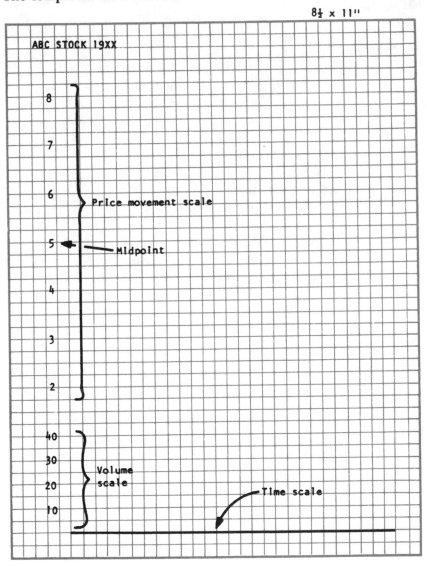

the way across the width of the paper with a pen. While this line will serve as the time scale for the chart, do not fill in any dates yet. Mark the date of each entry (or the date of each new week) as you do the chart.

Each column of boxes represents one trading day. If there is a holiday in the week, leave that column blank. Do not leave blanks for Saturdays and Sundays; that is what the heavy fifth line is for.

If you are using 8½ × 11" graph paper, you should be able to get six weeks' worth of trading on the sheet.

Volume Scale

About four or five boxes in from the left edge of the graph paper should be the first line on which you will make an entry. Do not darken this line, because you will be making an entry on it. This is the line, however, at which the time movement scale begins.

Leave about eight boxes above the time scale line for volume data. To calibrate this scale, you must know the range of volume in which the security trades. For example, if the volume averages 20,000 shares, the midpoint on the scale would be 20,000 shares (or just "20"). All volume scales must start at zero (flush with the horizontal scale), since it is possible—at least theoretically—that no trading, or close to none, could take place. On the upside, if actual volume is occasionally higher than your scale can accommodate, simply chart it on the same scale extended into the price movement part of the chart. The two may overlap. (You can avoid this happening often by going back over the stock's quotations for the prior several weeks, looking for a smoother average and possibly volume spikes.

A little trick is to use round numbers that are divisible by 4 or 5, such as 400, 800, 1,200 or 500, 1,000, 1,500. This just makes things easier.

Price Movement

You also have to take a midpoint of price movement. Either you can take the current quote from the newspaper and assume that it represents an average price, or you can go back over several weeks' worth of price movement history to determine a suitable midpoint. Once you have it, round the number off and plot it at the midway range above the volume scale. For example, if the average price of our stock were $5.125 (5⅛), then you would round that to 5 and put 5 at the midway point on the price movement part of the vertical axis. (For your convenience, Table 2-1 shows eighths and their equivalent dollar values in stock trading.)

TABLE 2-1 Eighths and their dollar values.

Point	*Dollar Value ($.000)*
1/8	.125
1/4	.250
3/8	.375
1/2	.500
5/8	.625
3/4	.750
7/8	.875
8/8 (1 point)	1.000

The next question is where do the other points go? For stocks under $15, the next whole number is best placed four 1/4″ boxes away. Each box represents a 1/4-point ($.250), and each half-box is an 1/8-point ($.125). For stocks trading over $15, make each box equal to 1/2-point.

Whether you mark each calibration on the price movement scale is up to you. After a while, you should become experienced enough to be comfortable with each whole point being marked.

The Worksheet

In addition to the bar chart itself, you should keep a worksheet, which contains the name of the security and all the information found in the newspaper quotes—date, day, volume, high, low, close, and change. The worksheet is important for reference purposes.

Exercise

The newspaper quote for XYZ is as follows:

52-Week High	*Low*	*Stock*	*Div*	*Yld %o*	*PE Ratio*	*Sales 100s*	*High*	*Low*	*Last*	*Chge*
14 3/4	7 5/8	FanPr	.66	5.4	16	28	12 3/8	12 1/8	12 1/8	−3/8

Now take a plain sheet of graph paper and create a chart for Fantasy Productions. Start by placing the name of the stock at the top left and the year.

TIME SCALE.   This will be a daily bar chart, to be used for as many weeks as the paper holds out. Come in about four or five boxes from the left edge of the sheet and up two boxes from the bottom. Draw the time scale line. (See Figure 2-5.)

FIGURE 2-5   The XYZ bar chart.

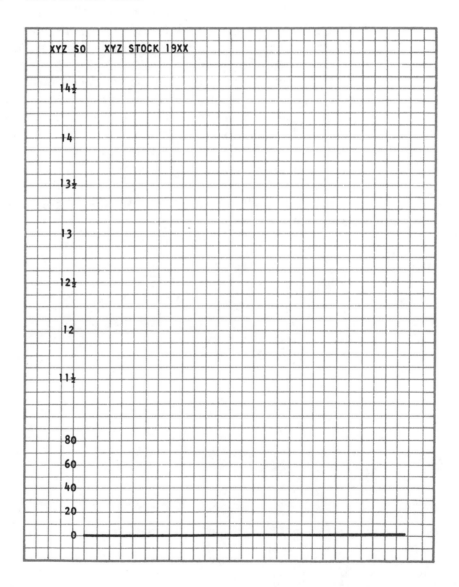

VOLUME SCALE.   According to the quotation, the volume is 28, that is, 28,000 shares, since the heading indicates that the entry is in thousands (Sales 100s). Count four boxes up from the left edge of the time scale and mark the line "40." Why 40? Because we can mark the next lower lines 30, 20, and 10, bringing us to zero at the time scale line. Also mark the preceding four grid lines 50, 60, 70, and 80.

PRICE MOVEMENT SCALE.   Since you know the high and low prices (12⅜ and 12⅛), you can devise a scale that accommodates this range. Suppose we set the low end of the price movement scale at 11—that is, mark the ninth line from the bottom "11"—and then make each box equal to ⅛-points ($.125). Assuming you have about 30 boxes left on the vertical axis, the topmost line should be 14¾ ($.125 a box times 30 boxes, plus the starting point, 11). You can mark either every second, third, or fourth box, depending on how much calibration makes you comfortable. If your chart paper has a heavy fifth line, use it to distinguis weeks (five trading days; weekends don't count). For instance, if you start a chart on Wednesday, count three lines in from a heavy line so as to synchronize the lines with the actual weeks. (See Figure 2-5 for the prepared chart.)

Exercise

Prepare a chart on your own from the following Friday quotations:

52-Week High	Low	Stock	Div	Yld ‰	PE Ratio	Sales 100s	High	Low	Last	Chge
12⅝	5⅞	FanPr	—	—	14	32	9⅛	9	9⅛	+⅛

When the chart is ready, compare it to the one in Figure 2-6. Try preparing other charts from the financial news until you feel competent.

FIGURE 2-6   The completed bar chart for Fantasy Productions. You might have
              placed the 9-point mark higher up on the price movement scale. That's
              fine. Also, you might have selected 30 or 35 as your midpoint on the
              volume scale, but can you divide the tick marks equally down to zero?

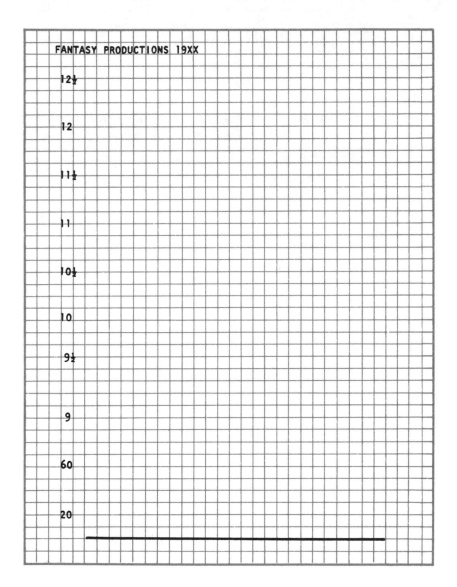

Inserting Price Data

Price data takes the form of a vertical bar (hence "bar" chart), which represents several types of information.

To construct a bar for a trading period, plot the high, low, and closing prices. (Sometimes the opening price is also plotted, but it is considered of much less value than the others.) Let's assume that, for a given stock, the high is 32⅞, the low is 32, and the closing is 32¼. The high and low prices are connected by a vertical line on the price movement scale. See Figure 2-7. The closing price is represented by a horizontal tick to the right side of the bar, at the appropriate point on the scale. If you wish to plot the opening price, you would make a tick to the left side of the bar.

**FIGURE 2-7
How a bar is
constructed.**

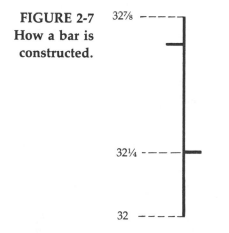

Exercise

Use the information for Fantasy Productions' quotation to make the first entry on your chart (use pencil). When you are done, compare your entry with the one in Figure 2-8.

FIGURE 2-8   The first price data entry on Fantasy Productions' bar chart.

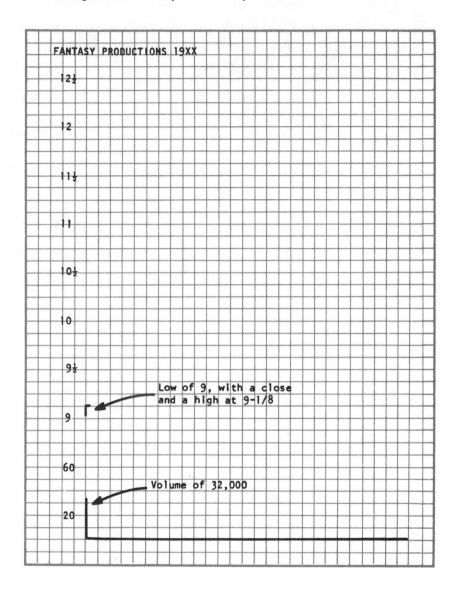

Charting for Futures Trading

The bar chart you've just constructed can be used for any security—equities, debt, options, currencies, and so on—as well as for futures contracts (which are, by the way, technically not securities). In futures trading, volume is also an important indicator, but it is defined a little differently. Also, "open interest" must be included on the chart.

- Volume is defined as total amount of trading activity expressed in terms of the total number of contracts traded for the day. It is recorded just as volume is on any other type of bar chart.

- Open interest is the total number of outstanding, or "open," contracts held by market participants at the close of trading. A futures contract is said to be "open" when it has not been liquidated by an offsetting transaction or fulfilled by delivery. When trading in a new delivery month begins, no contracts exist. Unlike a stock or bond, a futures contract is not "issued" by a corporation. Rather, it is created when a buyer and seller enter into a trade—an opening transaction. As the number of new transactions increases, so does the open interest, to which there is theoretically no limit. When a holder of a contract sells it, or when a short seller buys it back, or when a delivery is made on a contract, the open interest is offset by the so-called "closing transaction."

On a bar chart, open interest is represented by a continuous line running slightly above the volume scale. Some chart services also offer another line that represents average open interest levels for the period covered; these averages are made from previous years' data and are useful in pointing out seasonal fluctuations.

There are several things to note about volume and open interest.

First, during a trading day, futures volume can only rise, since it is a function of the number of transactions, whether they represent new positions or closeouts of existing positions. Open interest, on the other hand, can rise or fall during a trading day because it is the net of all remaining open contracts left after all opening and closing transactions are balanced out.

The volume scale and open interest line are for the total volume in a contract (such as gold or soybeans), not for individual con-

tracts (such as October gold or November soybeans). The reason
has to do with the normal life cycle of an individual contract. Both
open interest and volume rise from zero when a contract starts
trading, increase toward the middle of the expiration period, and
drop off as the contract nears expiration. This cycle is not a result of
supply and demand interaction, but rather a reflection of the
limited life of the futures contract. If your chart contained data only
on the specific contract's volume and open interest, this fluctuation
due to life cycle would reduce their value to little or zero.

In the futures section of the financial news, the volume and
open interest figures lag the price information by one day. For
example, Wednesday's paper will contain actual prices and esti-
mated volume for Tuesday's trading, along with official open
interest and volume figures for Monday. This lag results from the
time it takes to compile all the information and report it—by the
time it is on hand, the newspaper has been printed. For those who
are involved in day-to-day futures trading, this can present a
problem. If you intend to be that involved, you will want to
consider investing in an electronic on-line service that will get the
information to you sooner.

One final note: The financial news reports volume and open
interest in terms of the number of contracts, which you can use as
is when preparing your charts. For grain, however, these figures
are also reported in the newspapers in terms of contracts but in the
chart services in terms of bushels. So if you are charting a grain
contract, you must multiply by the number of bushels per contract
before entering volume on the chart. For example, if the newspaper states the volume as 10,000 (contracts), you must multiply by
5,000 (bushels per contract) and enter 5,000,000 on your chart.

Exercise

Before proceeding, prepare a bar chart from the following information (right out of the financial news) and make the entry for the day:

BRITISH POUNDS (IMM)—62,500 pounds; $ per pound

	Open	High	Low	Settle	Change	Lifetime High	Low	Open Interest
Sep	1.7052	1.7082	1.6994	1.7068	+38	1.9012	1.6506	14,938

Prior day's sales: 15,043 (that is, "Volume: 15,043 contracts")
Prior day's open interest: 20,779

When you are done, compare your chart with Figure 2-9.

FIGURE 2-9   Bar chart for British pounds futures contract. Notice how sensitive the price movement scale is with each box equal to one cent.

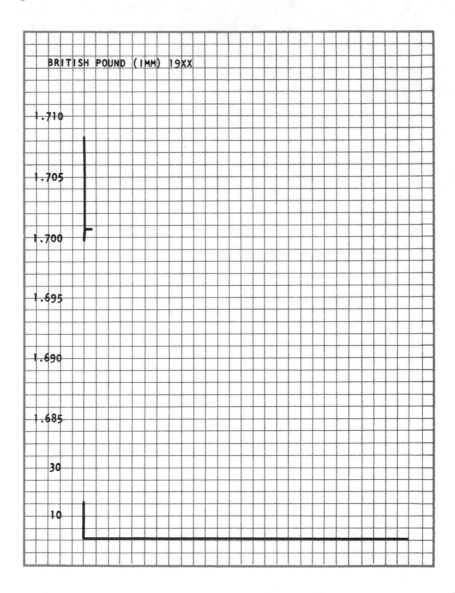

Note: If you are interested in charting futures, a suggested reading is John J. Murphy's *Technical Analysis of the Futures Markets* (New York: New York Institute of Finance, 1986).

Point and Figure (P&F) Charts

Point and figure charts were originally used for intraday trading, and beyond that application they are not widely used. One reason is that only rarely does a chart service offer P&F formats. Another is that keeping a P&F chart can be extremely tedious and time-consuming.

Paper Needed

The preferred paper for P&F charts is an 11 × 17" graph paper consisting of 10 squares per inch. A heavy fifth line is also desirable if you are making a daily chart. If the paper you are using does not have such a line, you might note a 0 (zero) or 5 at the foot of every fifth column; this notation is sometimes used to signify the end of a trading week.

Construction

The first step in preparing a point and figure chart is to lay out the 11 × 17" paper so that the vertical price movement scale runs up and down the leftmost 11" side. In the upper lefthand corner, block print the name of the security or futures contract to be charted and the appropriate date or dates.

Next, there are three decisions to be made when preparing a point and figure chart:

- Price movement scale.
- Box size.
- Reversal criterion.

PRICE MOVEMENT SCALE. This is simple, compared with what you must do for a bar chart. Simply pick a rounded number about the midpoint of the recent price range of the stock or contract. Assign that price to the middle of the vertical axis on your chart, and you're done.

BOX SIZE.   Before you can complete the price movement scale, you have to determine box size, that is, the value of each box. Perhaps the easiest thing to do is to assign the trading unit or some multiple of it. For example, for stocks the calibration would be in ⅛-points or multiples thereof. For futures, the trading unit of the contract might apply. For gold, each box would be worth ten cents, because for gold contracts ten cents is the minimum unit of fluctuation (that is, a contract's price may not go up or down, say, five cents).

If you use the minimum fluctuation or trading unit, then your chart will be very sensitive to price changes, and you will be very busy recording every price change. You might want to consider, depending on your needs, a larger box size, perhaps two, three, or more times the trading unit.

REVERSAL CRITERION.   Unlike a bar chart, in which each column of boxes represents a trading day, a P&F chart's column indicates a reversal in price movement. You move one column to the right and record the change every time there is a reversal, or "retracement," in prices. (How you do that will be explained shortly.) The question is what constitutes a reversal? What is the reversal criterion?

The reversal criterion is defined—by you—in terms of fluctuation or trading units. If you feel that a one-unit reversal is not enough to be regarded as a reversal, then the criterion might be two, three, or more. Assuming, for example, that you pick a two-unit criterion, then a countermovement of one unit would not be recorded on the chart; a countermovement of two or more would.

As you can see, the greater the number of units assigned as the criterion, the less sensitive the chart will be. With a criterion of three units, no fluctuations of one or two units would show on the chart. If such small ripples are not relevant to your objectives, then the criterion is acceptable. If they are important, then you have to consider the added work that goes into keeping a very sensitive chart with a one-unit criterion.

Box size and reversal criterion are important because point and figure charts are described in terms of these values. For example, a chart whose box size is one trading unit and whose criterion is three units is called a "1 × 3" chart. A 1 × 2 chart would be more sensitive, and a 2 × 4 chart would be less sensitive.

Exercise

The following numbers represent a week's worth of trading in Fantasy Productions stock:

Trading Day	High	Low	Close	Volume (000s)
Monday	9⅜	9	9¼	35
Tuesday	9⅝	9⅜	9½	42
Wednesday	9⅞	9¼	9⅞	50
Thursday	10⅛	9⅞	9⅞	45
Friday	10	9⅝	9¾	40

The previous Friday's close was 9⅛.

Take a sheet of graph paper, and mark it "Fantasy Productions" at the top left. Also note the starting date of the chart—pick the day of the month that coincides with a Monday.

Next select a midpoint for the price range. In this case, 9 or 10 will do. Assign this number to the middle box (not the line) on the vertical axis. Follow along by referring to Figures 2-10a-e.

Now what box size should we use? Since the stock trades under $15 (although it seems to be moving up), each box should probably be equal to an ⅛-point. Assigning even two trading units—that is, making a box equal to a ¼-point—would severely lessen the sensitivity of the chart.

What about the reversal criterion? Since the price movement range seems to be within two dollars, a fairly sensitive criterion is in order. Let's start with ⅛-point.

Our chart will therefore be a 1 × 1; that is, it will have a box size of 1 and a reversal criterion of 1. Mark "1 × 1" next to the date in the chart heading.

To actually chart the week's price movements, start by placing a dot in the box for 9⅛ (you can start a box or two in from the vertical axis if you wish). The 9⅛ figure represents the closing price of the preceding Friday. It is merely a starting point. (See Figure 2-10a.) To chart the week's worth of closing prices (only), use x's to represent upward price movements and o's to show downward movements:

FIGURE 2-10a Starting the Fantasy Productions' one-week, 1 x 1 P&F chart.

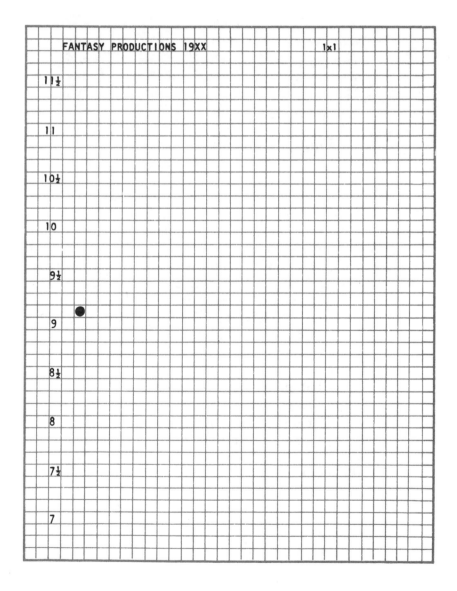

• For Monday, place one x in the box above, which represents a
rise in price to 9¼ on that day. (If the box size had been made
equal to a ¼-point, we would have made no notation for Monday
because the change would have been only an ⅛-point.) (See
Figure 2-10b.)

FIGURE 2-10b Monday's entry on the Fantasy Production's P&F chart.

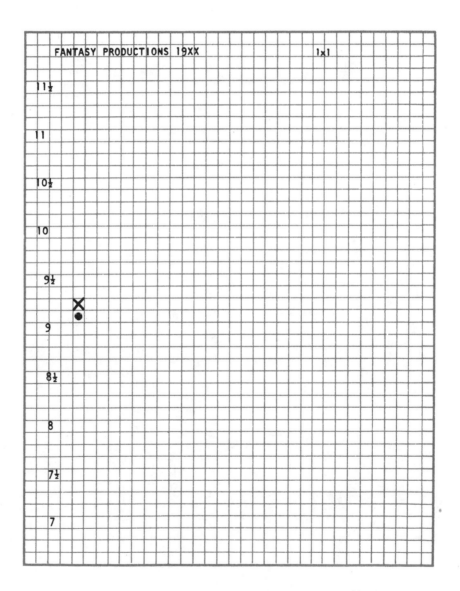

- For Tuesday, do not change columns. Instead, simply put two more x's above the first one to represent the continued upward price movement. (Remember that P&F charts do not reflect time. Trades could occur in five minutes or a week's time; a single column of figures could represent a whole week's worth of trades if they all move in the same direction or if the reversal criterion is not sensitive enough to detect minor retracements.) (See Figure 2-10c.)

FIGURE 2-10c Tuesday's entry on the Fantasy Production's P&F chart.

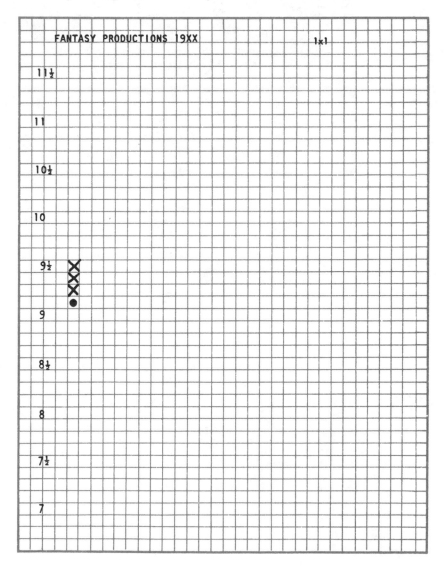

• For Wednesday, stay in the same column. Add three more x's to show the rise to a close at 9⅞. (See Figure 2-10d.)

FIGURE 2-10d Wednesday's entry on the Fantasy Production's P&F chart.

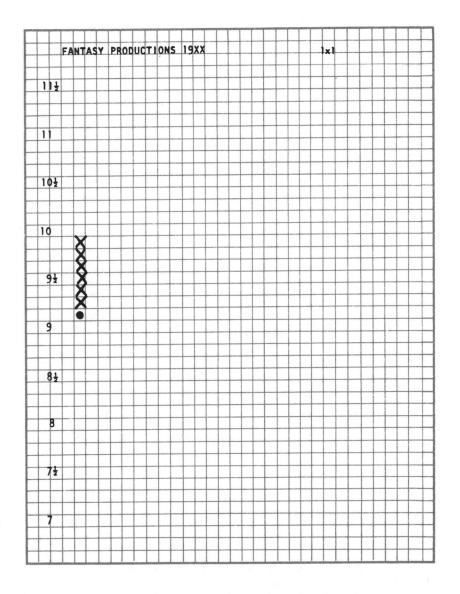

• For Thursday, make no notation at all. There is neither a price change nor a reversal. (Figure 2-10d remains the same.)

- For Friday, go to the next column, drop down one box and insert an o (for a downward movement) in the box for 9¾. Since there has been a reversal, you change columns. You drop down one box because that is the convention when changing columns; if it were a reversal of a downtrend, you would go up one box. (See Figure 2-10e.)

FIGURE 2-10e Friday's entry on Fantasy Production's P&F chart.

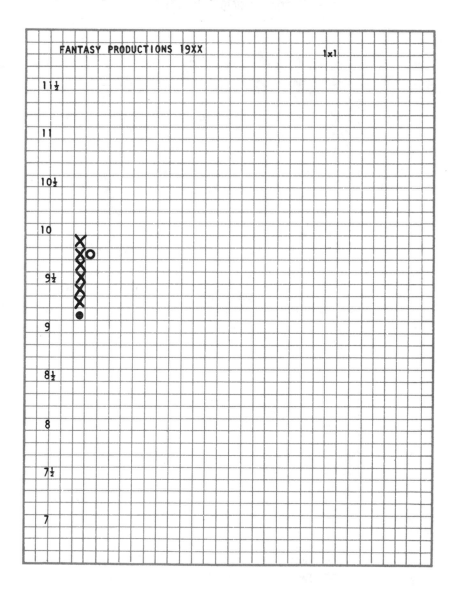

Exercise

Here is another week's worth of trades. Continue the chart in Figure 2-10. (Ignore volume for now.)

Trading Day	High	Low	Close	Volume (000s)
Monday	10⅛	9¾	10	42
Tuesday	10¼	10⅛	10⅛	50
Wednesday	9⅞	9	9⅞	54
Thursday	10¾	10½	10½	60
Friday	9⅝	9¼	9¼	38

Compare your chart with Figure 2-11.

FIGURE 2-11   Fantasy Productions's two-week, 1 x 1 P&F chart.

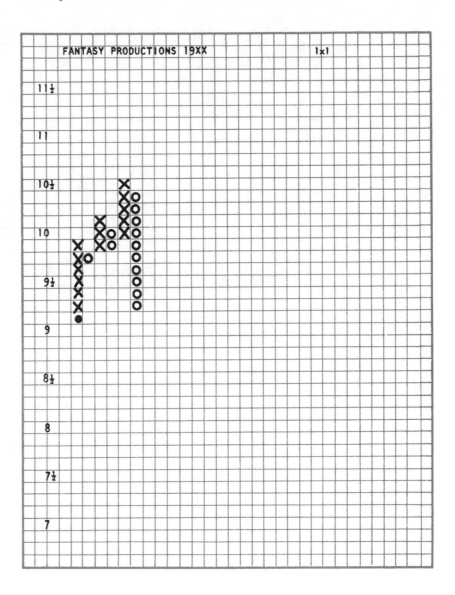

Exercise

Start a new sheet and make the chart a 1 × 2 and see how the configuration of the price movement changes. Check your results against Figure 2-12.

FIGURE 2-12   Fantasy Productions' two-week, 1 x 2 P&F chart.

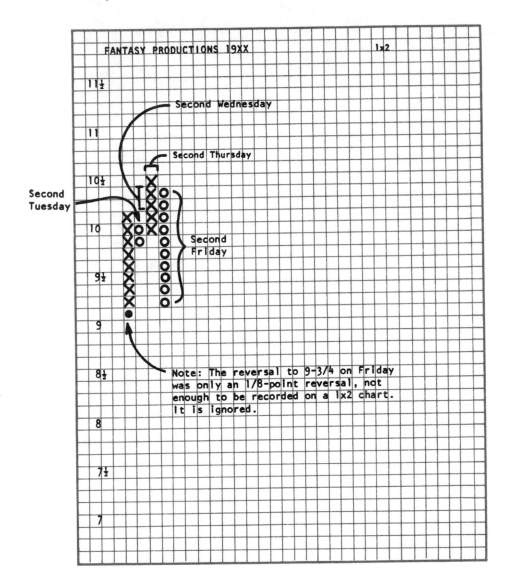

Exercise

Use the same data to plot two weeks' worth of trades on the bar chart in Figure 2-8 and compare your chart with the one in Figure 2-13.

FIGURE 2-13   Fantasy Productions' two-week bar chart.

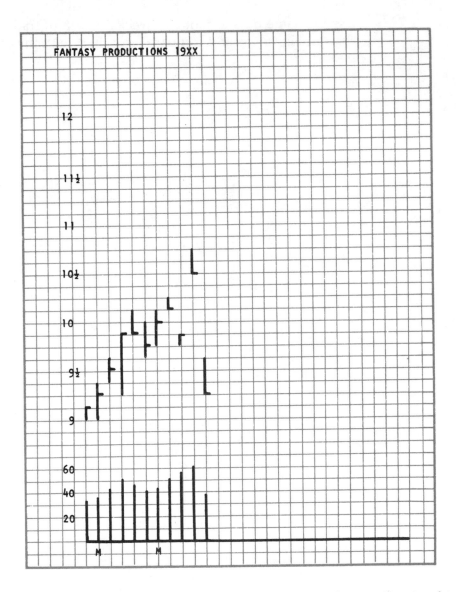

When you have completed the suggested exercises in this chapter, you might go on to start charts for actual stocks or contracts, using the financial news or other sources of information. Start doing that now, so that you have "real time" charts to look at when we explain how to interpret price action. This is what we will start to do in the next chapter, which deals with trends and trendlines.

3
Trends and Trendlines

Markets move not in perfectly straight lines, but through peaks and troughs. Prices move up, down, and even sideways; in fact, they move sideways about a third of the time. They may go up sharply or slowly, decline gradually or plummet. Amid all this activity, the technical analyst clings to two cardinal assumptions:

- Prices move in trends.
- Trends continue in direction until something acts on them to change their direction.

The operating principles are therefore that (1) if you can identify the trend with a fair degree of certainty, (2) you may assume the trend will continue, and (3) you can take the appropriate position in the market.

Now that you know how charts are prepared, and how to prepare them yourself, you are ready to draw trendlines. But where do you start? Although the day-to-day movements can change direction rapidly and frequently, the longer-term, overall direction can usually be perceived very readily. While traders may profit from in-and-out transactions on short-term fluctuations in a market, you, as an individual investor, are more likely to ignore the ripples and focus on the intermediate and major movements.

What are Trends?

Where, amid the zigzagging price movements, is the trend? What constitutes a trend? What do you look for?

• In an uptrend, look for a series of "ascending" highs and lows; that is, each peak or trough is higher than the one preceding. See Figure 3-1. The lows are called "reaction lows" because they run counter to the general trend.

**FIGURE 3-1
An uptrend.**

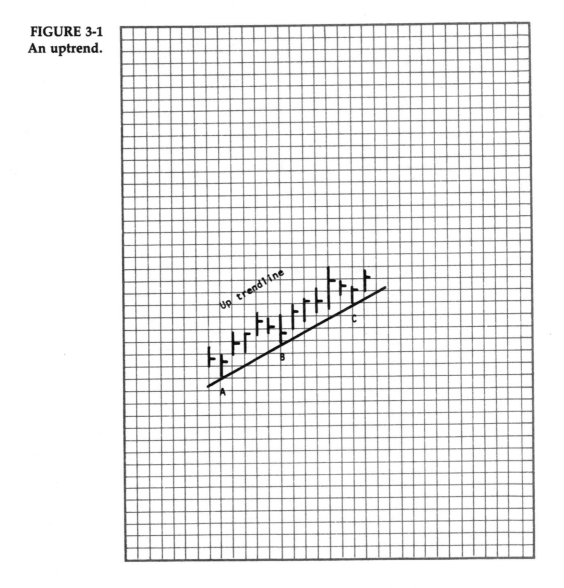

- In a downtrend, you will see a series of "descending" lows and highs; each peak or trough is lower than the one before it. See Figure 3-2. The peaks are sometimes called "reaction highs."

FIGURE 3-2   A downtrend.

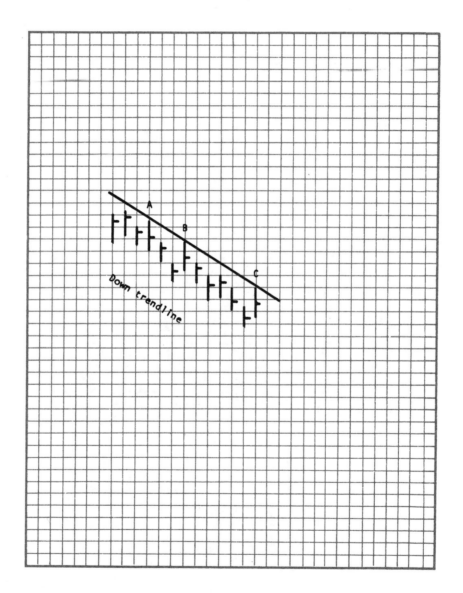

- In a sideways, or horizontal, market, highs and lows neither ascend nor descend. Prices rise and fall within a fairly constant band, called the "trading range." See Figure 3-3. Although a highly experienced analyst may detect signs that would indicate whether prices are going to move up or down, the future of a horizontal market is perhaps the most difficult projection to make in technical analysis.

FIGURE 3-3   A sideways, or horizontal, market.

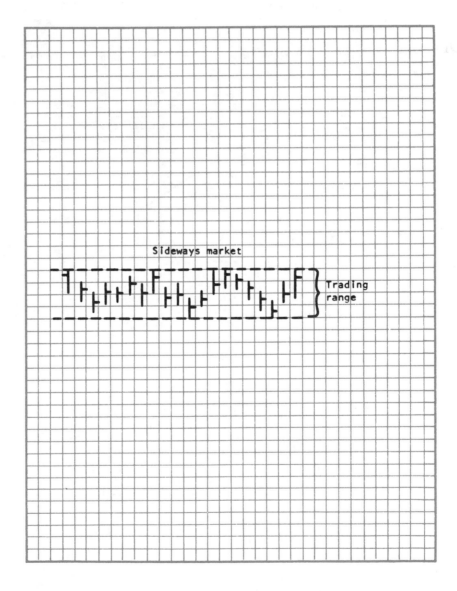

The "ideal" trend can be defined very specifically. An ideal uptrend is one in which each reaction low comes exactly the prior high: for example, starting with a low of 5, prices would move up to 10, down to 5, up to 15, down to 10, up to 20, down to 15, and so on. In an ideal downtrend, each reaction high comes to the prior low: starting with 20 a the latest low, prices move to 15, up to 20, down to 10, up 15, down to 5, up to 10, and so on. Although you are not going to find many such ideal trends, the closer an actual trend comes to this form, the more likely it is going to continue.

Drawing Trendlines

There are a few simple rules for drawing trendlines:

- You need to connect two points for a tentative trend and three to confirm it (that is, to be certain you have properly identified a trend).
- Draw as many tentative trendlines as you think are appropriate for a given chart, in pencil. Once a trendline is confirmed, ink it in.
- Draw trendlines between and through the two points, extending as far as you think is necessary.

You draw trendlines for up- and downtrends in basically the same way. For uptrends, connect two lowest peaks in a series. (See peaks A and B in Figure 3-1.) For downtrends, connect two peaks. (See peaks A and B in Figure 3-2.) Either trendline is confirmed when prices "bounce off" the extended trendline after a reaction low or high. (See point C in Figures 3-1 and 3-2.) If prices fall short of the trendline in either direction (that is, for example, if point C did not occur), the tentative trendline stands, but it is not confirmed. If prices penetrate the trendline, you must adjust the line because now you have two new highs or lows. (See Figures 3-4 and 3-5.)

For a sideways market, you draw two lines: one connecting the two highest price points and the other connecting the two lowest. (See Figure 3-3.) Sideways markets are the least significant from a forecasting point of view, since it is difficult to foresee which way prices will break out of such a formation.

FIGURE 3-4   **An adjusted up trendline.**

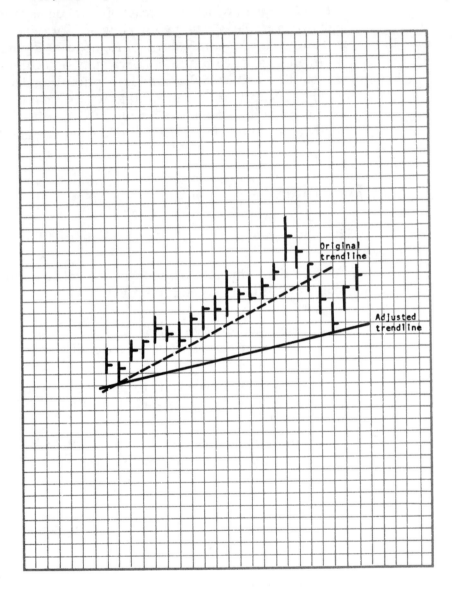

FIGURE 3-5   An adjusted down trendline.

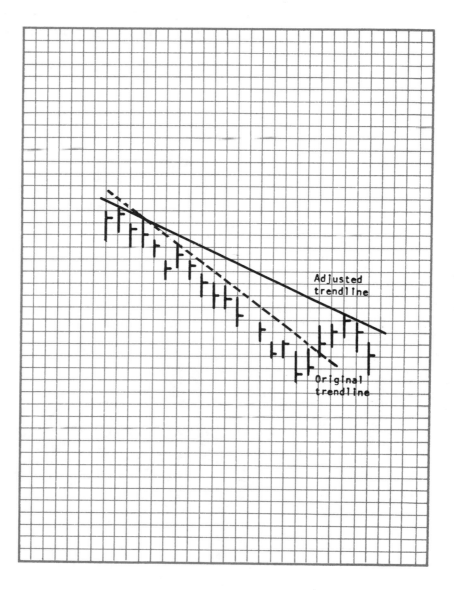

Exercise

In Figures 3-6, 3-7, and 3-8, identify the trends by drawing in the trendlines (in pencil). Then compare your results with Figures 3-9, 3-10, and 3-11.

FIGURE 3-6   Exercise.

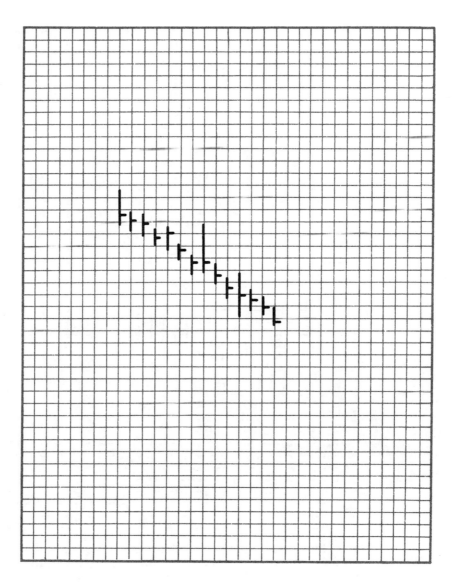

FIGURE 3-7   Exercise.

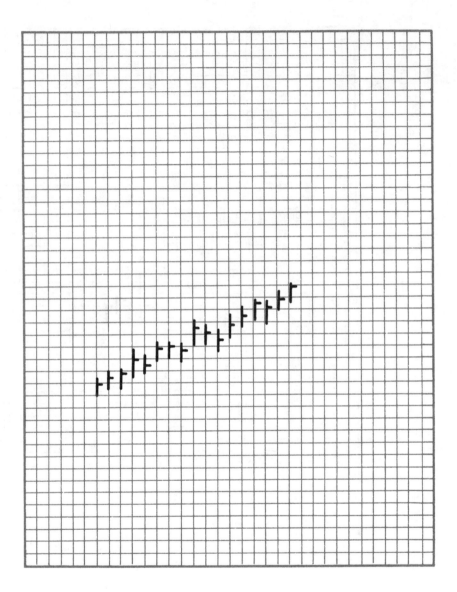

FIGURE 3-8   Exercise.

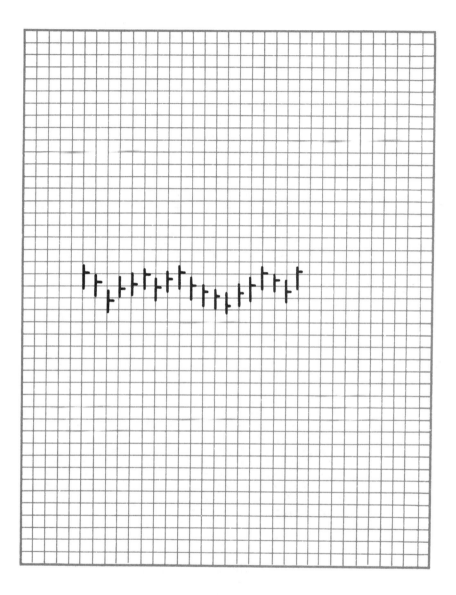

FIGURE 3-9   Answer to exercise.

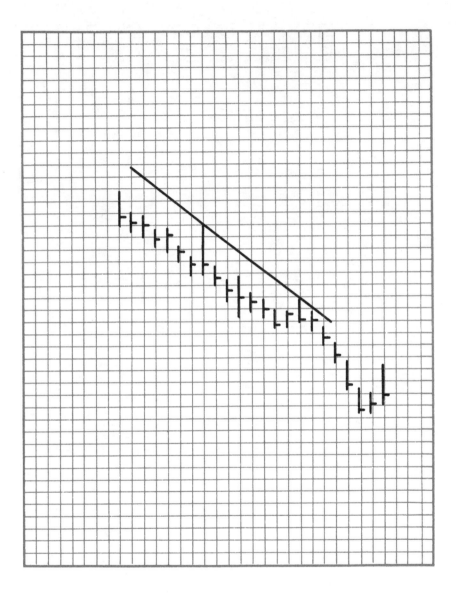

FIGURE 3-10   Answer to exercise.

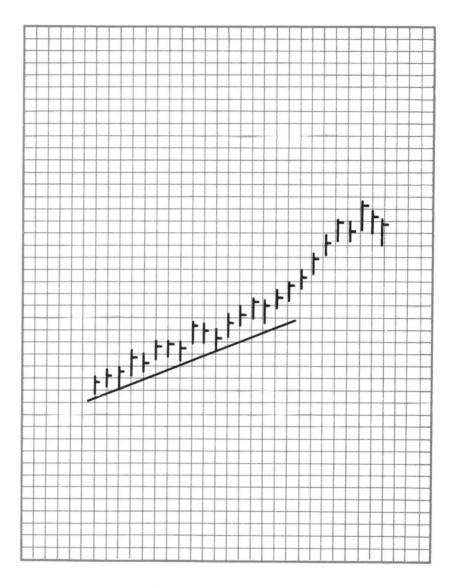

FIGURE 3-11   Answer to exercise.

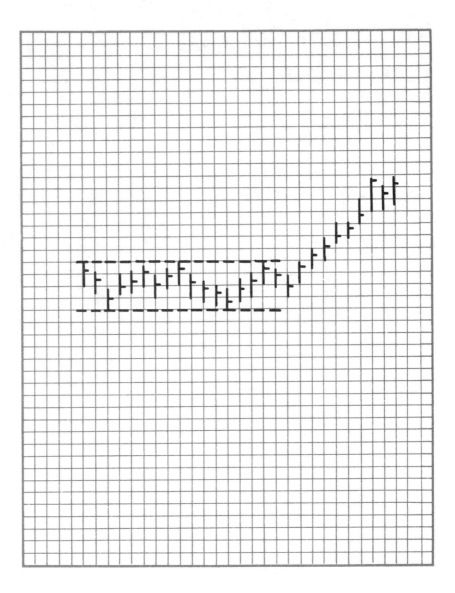

Exercise

Notice that Figure 3-9, 3-10, and 3-11 contains extended price action. Reevaluate your trendlines in the light of the new data.

- Which trendlines are confirmed?
- Which have to be adjusted?
- Is there any movement on the charts that you do not know how to handle?

Compare your confirmed or adjusted trendlines with those in Figures 3-12, 3-13, and 3-14. The movement in Figure 3-14 from point A to point B is a "breakout" from the trading range, but does it signal the beginning of a major uptrend?

FIGURE 3-12   Answer to exercise.

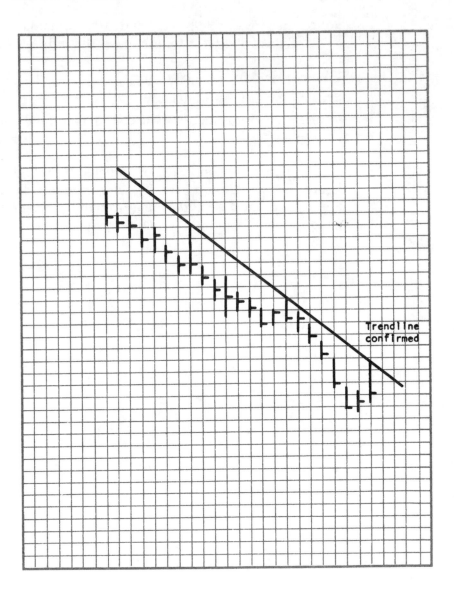

FIGURE 3-13 Answer to exercise.

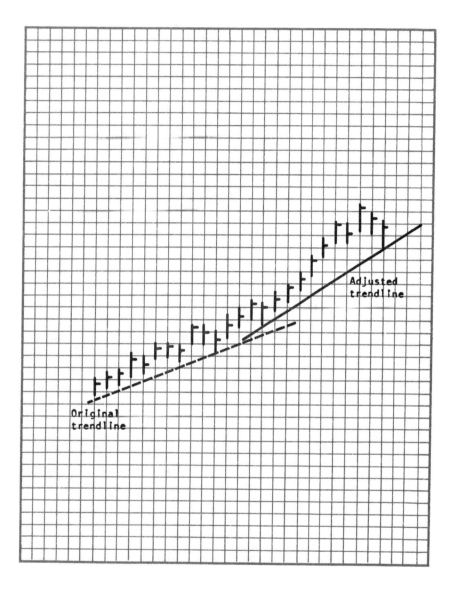

FIGURE 3-14   Answer to exercise.

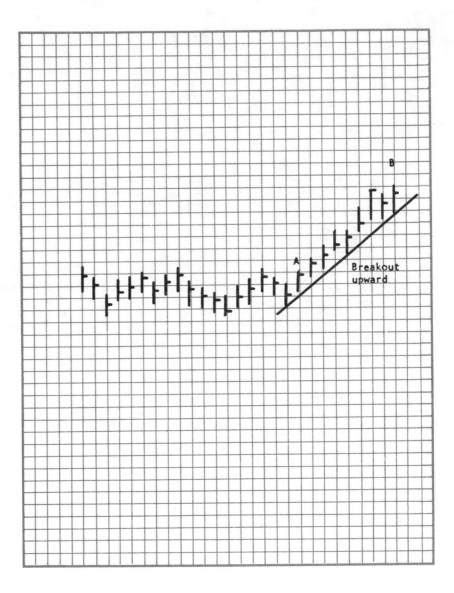

While your judgment is perhaps the most critical factor in answering this question, there are guidelines that you can use. For example, an intraday penetration, with the close within the trendline, is usually not significant. A closing price beyond the trendline is more important but not decisive. You could also use "filters," which are penetration criteria. For example, you might say that a closing price 3% beyond the trendline may be considered a signal of a reverse; this is a "price filter." Or you might say that any two consecutive closing prices outside the trendline indicate a reversal; this is a "time filter." Filters help you to quantify the basis for your decision making.

Retracements

Every trend has countermovement within it. The trick is in not letting a temporary countermove make you think it is a reversal in trend. If the countermove is a retracement, you will position yourself on the assumption that the interrupted trend will continue. If the countermove ia reversal, your position will reflect a change in trend. Being "faked" by a retracement can be fatal to your investment position.

Many countermovements, or retracements, can extend up to 50% of the last move in the direction of the trend. For example, let's say that a stock moves from a trough of 50 to a peak of 100, after which it starts moving downward. How far down may the price go before you have to start considering the countermovement a reversal? Most retracements extend to 50%, in this case to 75 (50% of the recent upward move from 50 to 100). The general retracement range is from one-third to two-thirds of the preceding move. In our example (see Figure 3-15) the range extends from about 83 (one-third) to about 66 (two-thirds).

What does this mean to you? In a very strong uptrend, you might be able to identify a "buying range" below the market (or a "selling range" above the market in a downtrend), whenever prices retrace to between one-third and one-half the preceding movement. If you do take a position and the market then retraces through the two-thirds level—either up or down—you know enough to cut your losses and get out.

These are basic guidelines on retracements. For more complex analytical methods, see the Bibliography at the end of the book.

FIGURE 3-15   Example of retracement.

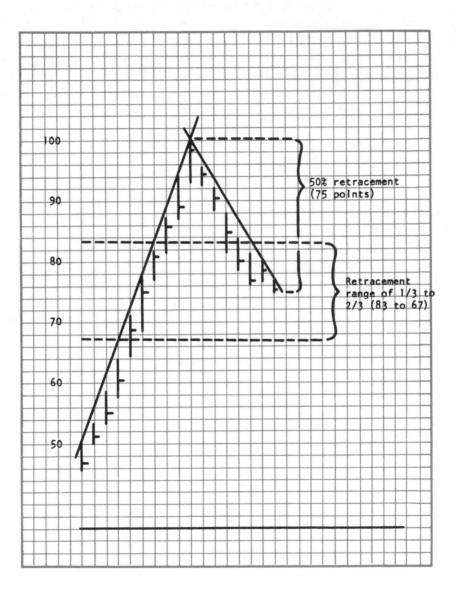

Channel Lines

Another useful tool is the channel line, which can sometimes be drawn as a line running parallel to the trendline at the opposite side of the trend. For example, in Figure 3-16, the trendline is the solid line drawn below the market, and the channel line is the dashed line drawn above the market. First establish the trendline; then draw a parallel line through the first peak (or trough in a downtrend). Subsequent movements away from the trendline should "bounce off" the channel line, which for this reason is sometimes known as the "return line."

FIGURE 3-16 Trend- and channel lines.

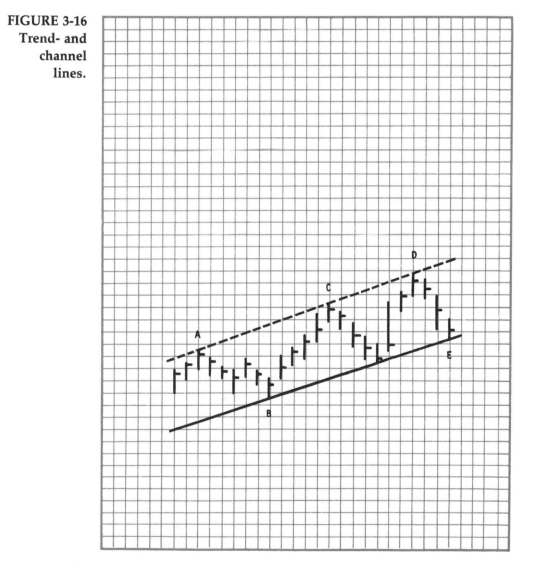

Exercise

In Figures 3-17 and 3-18:

- Draw the trendlines and channel lines, if any exist. (Draw the channel lines as dashed lines.)
- Identify buying and selling points.

Compare your results with Figures 3-19 and 3-20.

FIGURE 3-17 Exercise.

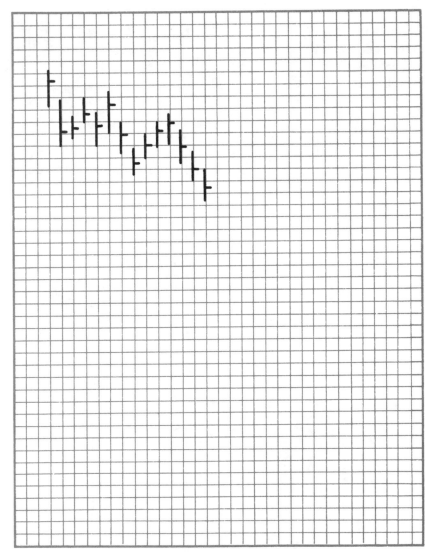

FIGURE 3-18 Exercise.

FIGURE 3-19   Answer to exercise.

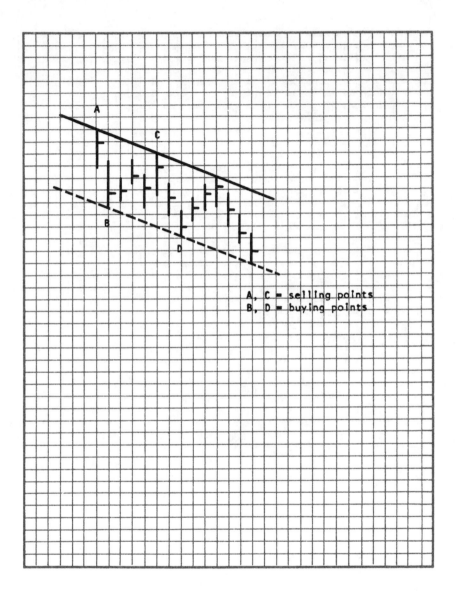

A, C = selling points
B, D = buying points

FIGURE 3-20   Answer to exercise.

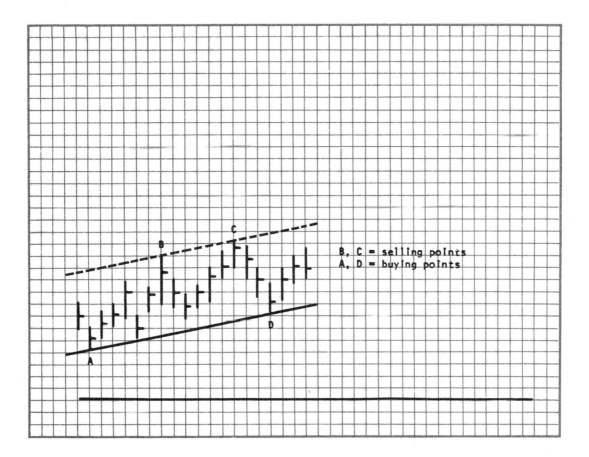

B, C = selling points
A, D = buying points

Do "real" price movements behave in this fashion so perfectly? No, but some come fairly close. The price action of an actively traded stock with a large float will often permit the drawing of a channel line. The reason is probably that there are enough buyers and sellers in the market for the reactions to price increases or declines to occur at the same levels over and over again.

Whatever the reason, the presence of a channel line is very helpful. The more often a return line is tested, the more valuable and reliable it becomes. Some aggressive traders even take positions counter to the market at the point where prices touch the channel line; this tactic can be very profitable if it works—and extremely costly if it does not. Nevertheless, once a reliable channel line is confirmed, the buy and sell points are easy to see.

Even when prices do not touch the return line, the information is useful, since such a failure is usually a sign that the trend is weakening and may even signal a breaking of the trendline. If prices move beyond a channel line, you may be seeing a strengthening trend. The adjusted channel line can then be used to accurately adjust the trendline. Channel lines have measuring value too. The simple rule is that, once prices break out of the channel line, they are likely to move at least the width of the channel.)

Exercise

Figures 3-21 through 3-22 are continuations of the charts in Figures 3-17 through 3-18. For each of these figures:

- Determine whether the channel line is still valid or should be adjusted in some way.
- Draw, as necessary, the adjusted trendlines and channel lines.
- Identify buying and selling points, if any.

Compare your responses with those in Figures 3-23 through 3-24.

FIGURE 3-21   Exercise.

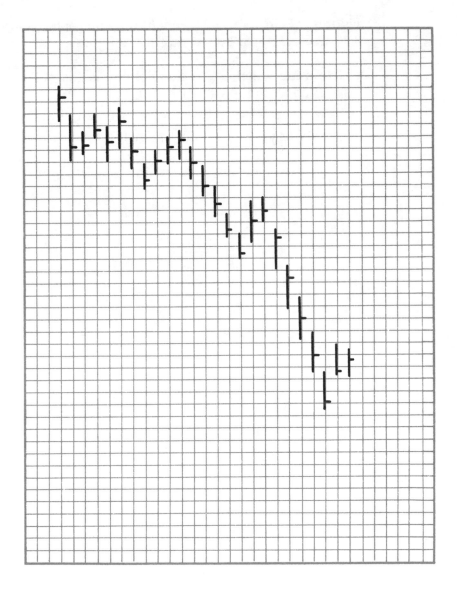

FIGURE 3-22   Exercise.

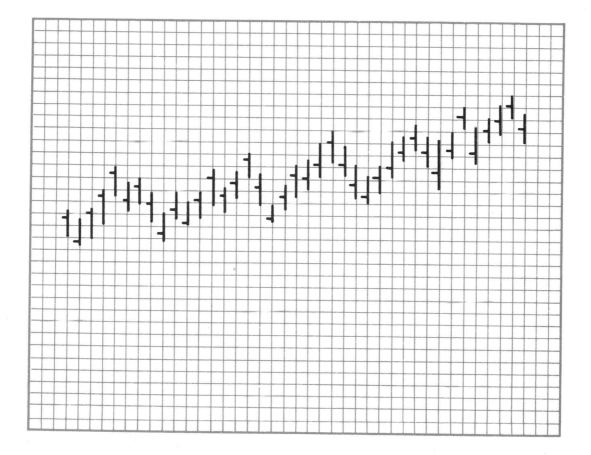

FIGURE 3-23   Answer to exercise.

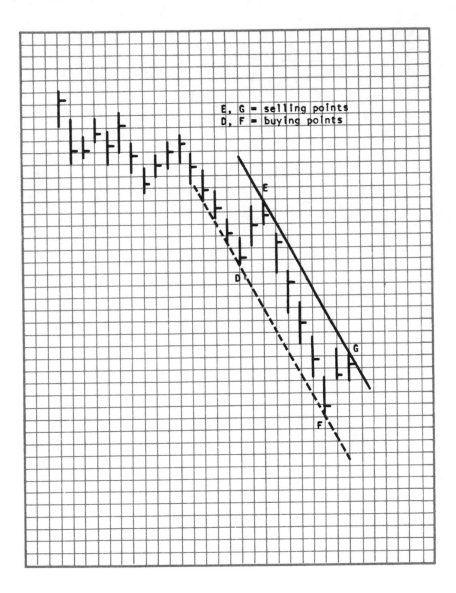

FIGURE 3-24 Answer to exercise.

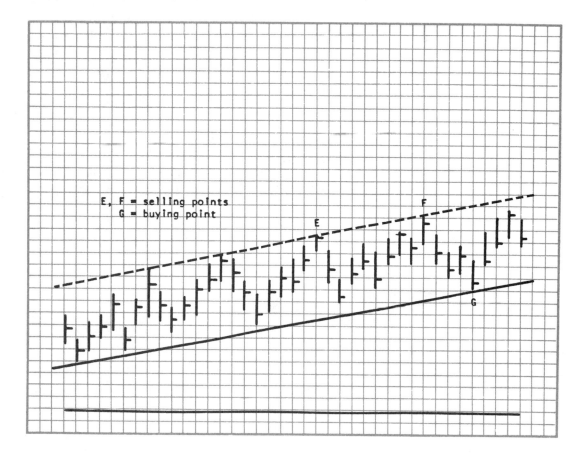

When you have completed these exercises, go over the charts that you have been creating (or those from a subscription service) to see whether trends and/or channels are developing. In the next chapter, we will talk a little more about how prices behave and why.

4

The Longs, the Shorts, and the Uncommitted

Prices change directions for many reasons, but the dominant influence consists of the expectations and desires of the market participants, who fall into three categories:

- The longs.
- The shorts.
- The uncommitted.

Any of these participants can affect price action. For example, in an uptrend, the longs are content but wish they had bought more. The shorts are becoming increasingly convinced that they are wrong and are looking for the chance to get out of the market. Of the uncommitted group, some never took positions but wish they had, while others sold off but wish they had not. All four groups are watching the market for a downturn, with an eye toward buying. Should the market dip, all four could become buyers and create enough demand to force prices up again. This leads us to the all-important definitions of support and resistance.

Support and Resistance

When declining prices meet with such demand and bounce back, they have hit "support." The result is a price dip—a "trough" or "reaction low." Support is therefore a level or area below the market where buying interest is strong enough to overcome selling pressure. (See Figure 4-1.)

FIGURE 4-1   An example of support.

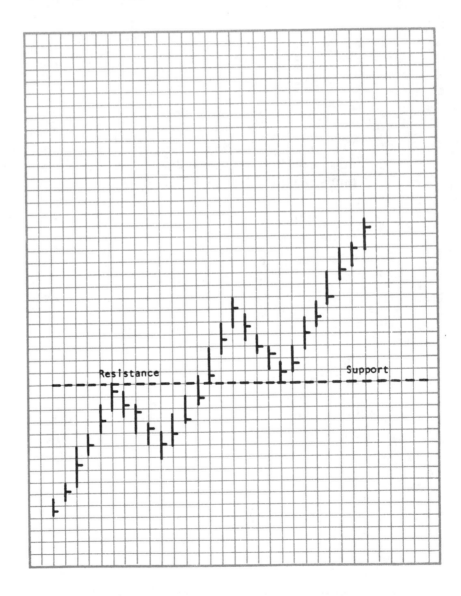

Resistance—the opposite of support—is a level or area above the market at which selling pressure overcomes buying interest. For example, let's say that prices are trending downward. The longs are looking for a chance to sell, and shorts are waiting to increase their positions. The uncommitted are likely to go short. Should the market turn upward, all four groups are likely to turn into sellers, thereby creating supply and causing prices to turn down again. The upturn and drop, on the chart, is referred to as a "peak" or "reaction high." (See Figure 4-2.)

FIGURE 4-2   An example of resistance.

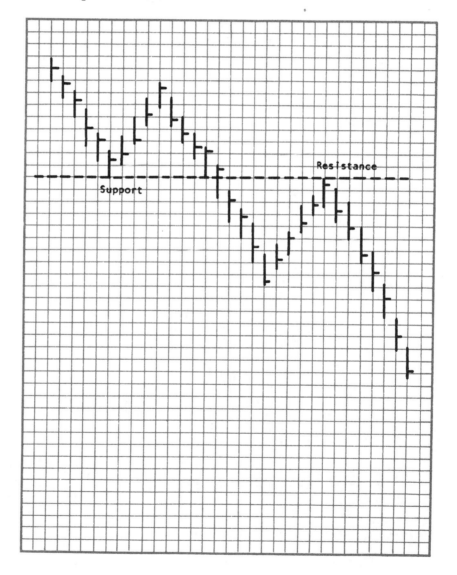

The most important thing to remember about support and resistance is that, once penetrated, they usually reverse their roles. For example, see Figure 4-3, in which prices test the 50 level three times, bouncing back to the 60-70 range between the troughs. If prices were to move down again, this time through the 50 level to, say, 40, they are said to have "broken their support." It is likely that a trend reversal is in the making. Should prices turn upward again toward the 50 level, they may very well bounce back off into a decline. Why? The previous support level at 50 becomes resistance. If the support penetrated was part of a minor trend, look for a reversal in the intermediate trend.

FIGURE 4-3   Support becomes resistance. (Note: For wide patterns, we've turned the sheet on its 11″ side; you would actually attach one upright sheet to another.)

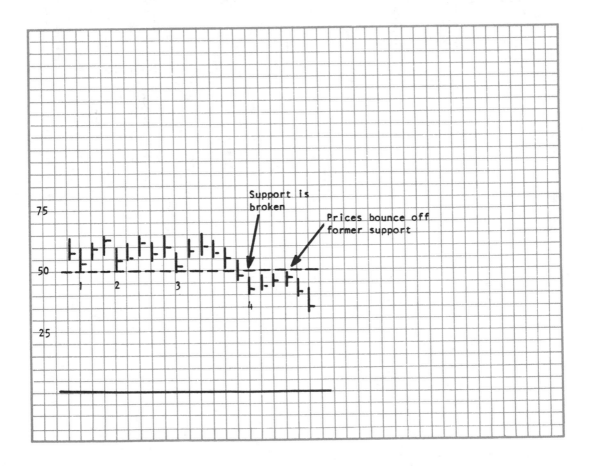

Similarly, resistance can become support. For example, suppose prices advanced to 50 more than once, dropped back to 35, and then moved up again to 55 (see Figure 4-4). They have broken through the resistance area—of 50, which becomes the support level. Why not 35? The reason is that resistance and support, once penetrated, reverse their roles. In this case, 50 was the resistance area penetrated, and it becomes the new support level.

FIGURE 4-4   Resistance becomes support.

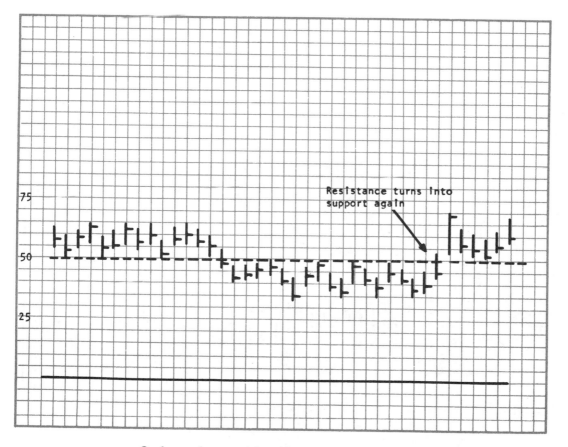

So how do you identify support and resistance levels? When they are in the making, you will note prices reversed fairly consistently at a certain price level. If they retreat from that level, you are looking at a resistance area. If they repeatedly advance from the same level, think in terms of support. Once you have identified a zone and it is penetrated, you may generally assume that it will reverse its role. Don't look elsewhere for a level.

Exercise

In Figures 4-5 and 4-6, identify the support and/or resistance zones (represented by lettered dashed lines). Compare your responses to Figures 4-7 and 4-8.

FIGURE 4-5   Exercise.

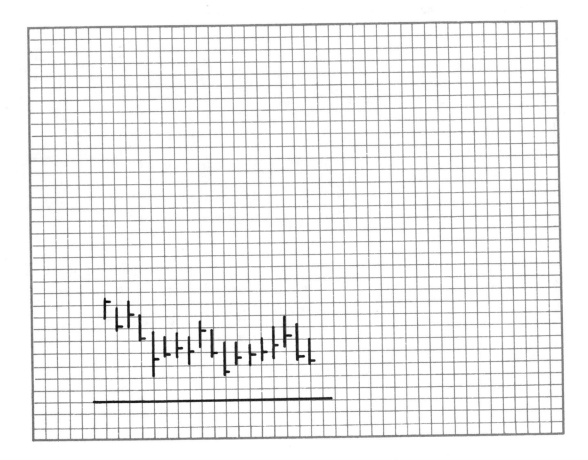

FIGURE 4-6   Exercise.

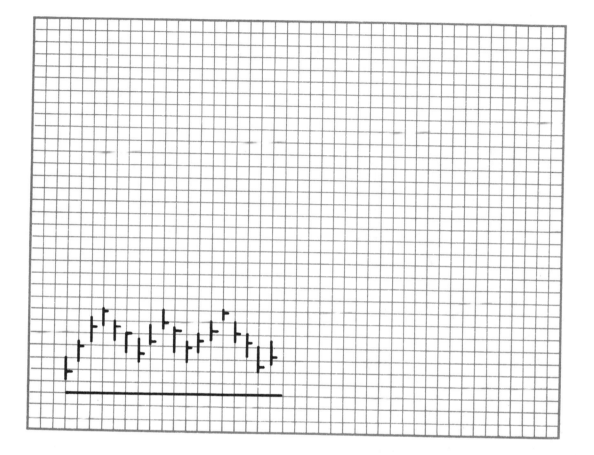

FIGURE 4-7   Answer to exercise.

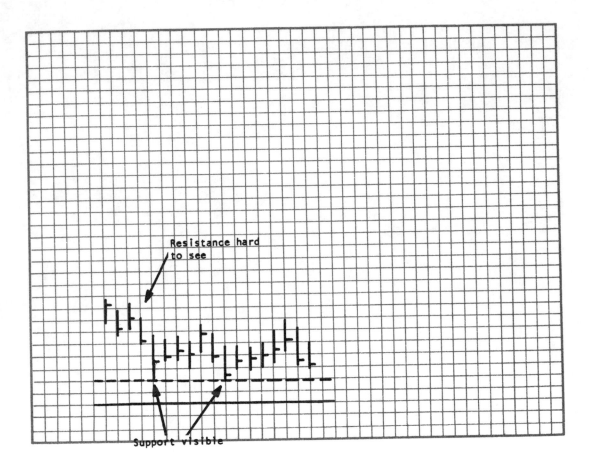

FIGURE 4-8   Answer to exercise.

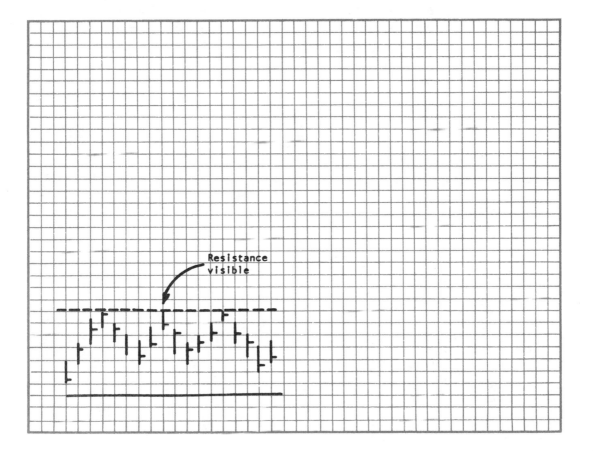

Exercise

In Figures 4-9 and 4-10, identify which points are resistance-turned-support or support-turned-resistance. Compare your responses with the charts in Figures 4-11 and 4-12.

FIGURE 4-9   Exercise.

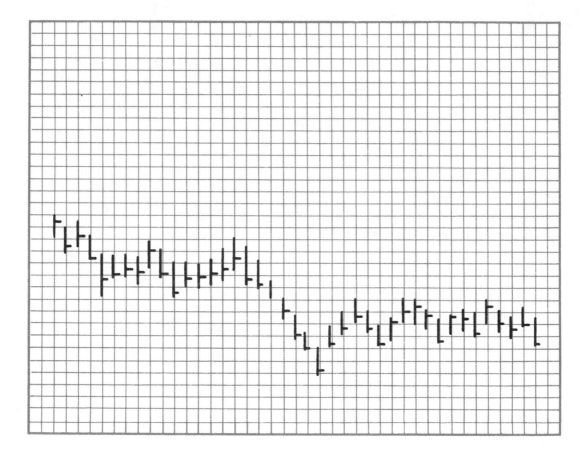

FIGURE 4-10   Exercise.

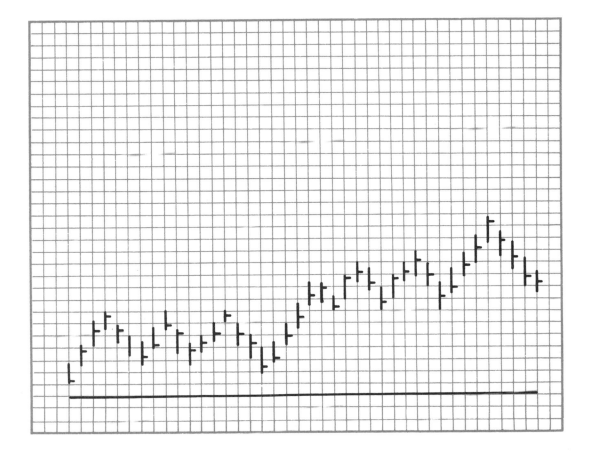

FIGURE 4-11   Answer to exercise.

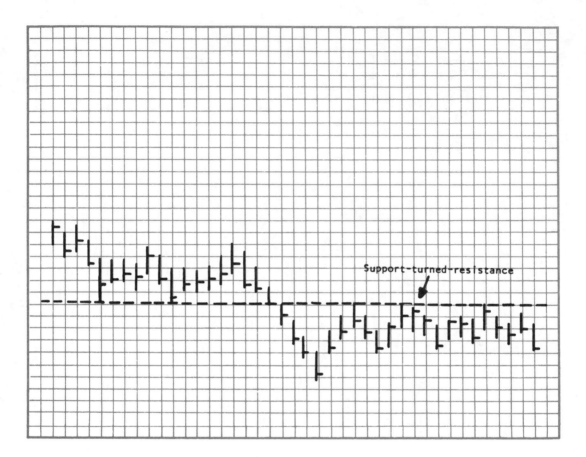

FIGURE 4-12   Answer to exercise.

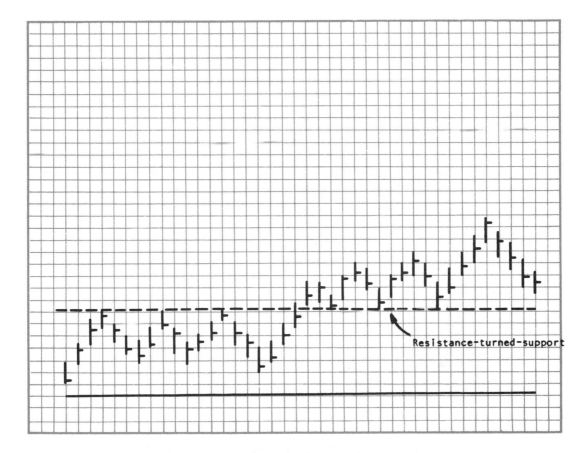

The examples so far have been pretty simple. Naturally, charting is not that easy. Identifying support and resistance is actually trickier than these illustrations would lead you to believe. In general, three conditions influence where support or resistance can develop:

- Volume.
- Extent of the movement prior to penetration.
- Time elapsed since the penetration.

Volume

Volume is a key indicator of the "strength" of a level. For example, if support or resistance occurs repeatedly at the same levels on high volume—thousands of shares or contracts—that area may be relied on much more than one characterized by low volume. Also, a single, sharp, high-volume deflection off a support or resistance area is much more significant and reliable than a series of short, low-volume tests. In general, high volume is an indication of reliability. Why? The formation of these levels depends on the great majority of market participants reacting in enough of a uniform way to make the pattern on the chart distinct. Heavy volume means a consensus among a large number of participants and therefore clear formations of levels. Low volume means there aren't that many players to start with—and probably not enough to establish a strong level of support or resistance.

Prior Movement

Let's try a little more complicated example of support-turned-resistance. Note the pattern of the stock in Figure 4-13: 20 to 30, 30 to 19, a little sideways activity with a support level established at 19, to 24, and then a a penetration through the support level. How far prices move down past the support level will influence where the resistance level is set. If they drop to, say, 17 before turning up again to 24, you probably will not see very much selling pressure at 19. Holders of the stock are just not that disappointed; many are likely to hold the stock in anticipation of further price increases. Resistance would not be likely to develop until about the 24 level.

If the decline had reached the 15 mark, however, you would have seen heavier "disappointed" selling at 19. Resistance could occur close to that level.

Assuming a plunge to, say, 10 or 12 with a subsequent rebound to 19, resistance would very probably develop quickly at 19, with many "disgusted" buyers glad to get out with as small losses as possible.

The general principle here is that, when support or resistance changes roles, its level is partly a function of the length of the prior movement. In our example, the reversal is from support to resistance and the "prior movement" is the decline from 24. A short

FIGURE 4-13   Example of support-turned-resistance. But where is the resistance?

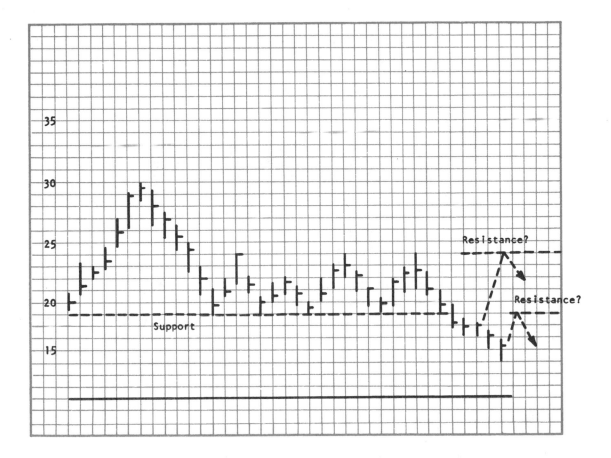

decline to 17 or so means a higher-level reistance. Progressively longer declines would mean lower areas. The same principle applies to resistance-turned-support.

As a corollary to this principle, determining reliable support and resistance levels for low- and medium-priced stocks can be difficult. For example, if a $5 stock declines to $4, that is a 20% drop in price—but it represents only $1. On a round lot, that's $100. Holders of the stock haven't been "stung" enough, in terms of dollars, to create, collectively, a resistance level. Take the same percentage of loss in value, from $125 to $100, and the resistance will become very evident when and if the stock swings upward again.

Time Elapsed Since Penetration

In general, the longer prices take to turn back through the point of penetration, the weaker the resistance or support will be. As always, these levels result from the psychology of the players in the market. In the case of a price downturn, the concomitant loss in value may lose its sting as time goes by. Perhaps holders perceive value in the stock as time goes by, despite the loss. Perhaps conditions in the economy or in the industry change favorably for the stock. So as the prices turn upward again after a long downturn or after prolonged sideways activity at a low, don't expect resistance to be as strong as if prices had dropped and picked up again sharply.

Also, if the level is tested frequently and gently over time, it tends to lose strength. For example, suppose, after a somewhat lengthy downtrend, prices turn upward several times, each time on low volume, only to rebound downward again. When prices eventually do test the resistance zone on heavy volume, the selling pressure is not likely to be very strong; it has been "soaked off" by the preceding numerous tests.

Although experienced chartists are sensitive to these and many other clues to support and resistance, such signals serve only as a basis for your personal judgment.

Gaps

All the charts used so far show a continuous price activity. That is, the successive price ranges reflected by the bars on the chart always overlap. Sometimes, however, on a daily bar chart, the highest price of one day does not overlap with the lowest price of the next day—in both up- and downtrends. (On intraday charts, opening and closing prices are not used, but prices can still "jump" from one range to another.) The result is a gap, which arises from an imbalance in supply and demand.

A "gap" is therefore a price range in which no trades take place. It occurs in an uptrend when the highest price of one day is lower than the lowest price of the next day. (See Figure 4-14.) In a downtrend, it appears when one day's lowest price is higher than the next day's highest price. (See Figure 4-15.)

FIGURE 4-14   Gaps in an uptrend.

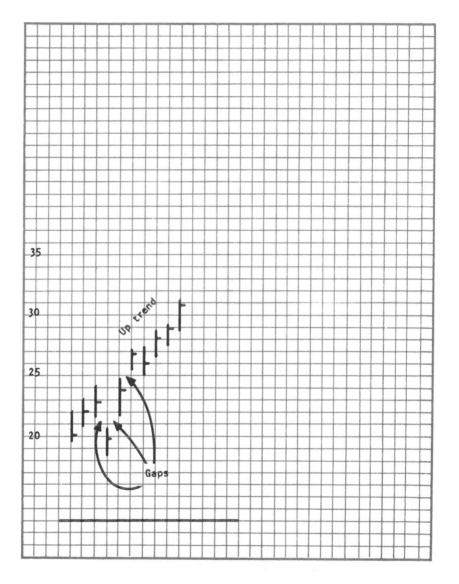

Perhaps the greatest misconception is that gaps must always be "closed," that is, retraced by price movement. Some chartists, given this belief, use any gap as a signal to take a position assuming that prices must close the gap. Such an assumption is by and large true: Sooner or later, a gap is usually closed—but there is no guarantee as to when it will be closed. Meanwhile, if you are sitting

FIGURE 4-15   Gaps in a downtrend.

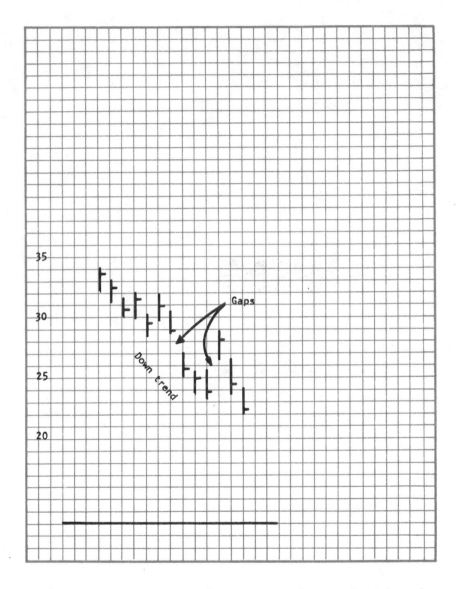

on a short position—waiting for a gap to close and paying the
interest expenses on the borrowed stock—you may lose in costs
more than you will gain by the time prices retrace the gap.

Gaps therefore should not be taken blindly as signals. While
some types of gaps have significance, others are meaningless. For
example, the intraday gap is not recorded on a daily bar chart; no

one preparing a daily chart is the wiser, and no one seems to lose out for the want of knowing about it. (Incidentally, gaps do not show up on a point and figure chart, only on a bar chart.) Another example is the gap that occurs when a stock goes ex-dividend; this is a reflection of the add-on value of the dividend to the stock's market value, which is determined by supply and demand.

The important thing to remember is that gaps reflect supply and demand, but they do not change the balance between selling and buying pressures. You must determine what the particular type of gap is saying about price movement. For example, a gap of 1/8-point in a high-priced, actively traded stock may be quite normal and reasonable. And meaningless gaps occur all the time in thinly traded stocks; they are merely a result of the sporadic trades in that security.

Types of Gaps

There are four basic types of gaps:

- Common (or area).
- Breakaway.
- Continuation (or runaway).
- Exhaustion.

COMMON (OR AREA) GAP.   This type of gap usually appears within trading or price congestion areas, near tops and bottomes of formations. Their technical significance is practically nil, except that they imply a congestion formation. For example, suppose prices move from 20 to 24, back to 18, and then to 32, with a gap somewhere in the last move. Prices are likely to move back through the 26-to-30 range, with the gap closed fairly quickly, unless it occurs on the final "crossing" of the congestion zone.

This type of gap generally means that, despite the presence of indecisive price activity, the prior trend will continue rather than reverse itself. What this means is that sometimes prices stop moving in the direction of their current trend. Instead, they move a little up, a little down—but not definitively in either an up- or a downtrend—before returning to their original direction. This type of activity is called "backing and filling," "consolidation," or a "continuation pattern." (If prices change direction after such activity, they are said to have undergone a "reversal.") The common gap therefore often occurs in consolidations, and so you have some indication that the original trend will continue sooner or later.

BREAKAWAY GAP.   Of more technical significance than the common gap, this type of gap typically occurs toward the completion of a pattern, just before prices "break away." For example, let's say a stock is consistently trading up to 36 and then falling back, but with a lot of selling pressure (heavy volume). What's happening is that most holders are selling at 36, thus offsetting buying pressure and creating conditions in which prices drop back down. Other holders, seeing prices come up to 36 and fall away, do one of two things: Either they drop their prices to below 36, or they wait for better prices. The result is an absence of sellers at the 36 level—a gap in the trading. Buyers have to then bid up past the 36 level to open or increase their positions. As buying pressure builds, prices get ready to "break away" past the resistance level at 36. (See Figure 4-16.)

While breakaway gaps usually accompany upside breakouts, they are not recorded as often as they occur because they are typically intraday. When you do see them, however, they are generally not false moves; they mean a breakout is coming. They arise from a stronger buying pressure than if no gap occurs; buyers have had to step up their bids considerably to find sellers. Prices can therefore be expected to go farther and faster once the breakout occurs.

Whether this gap is closed (within a reasonable amount of time) depends largely on volume. If the volume is greater before the gap than after, then it will probably be closed. If the preceding volume is lighter, it probably will not.

CONTINUATION (RUNAWAY OR MEASURING) GAP.   As prices advance rapidly, they gather momentum for days to weeks as demand steps up. After a while, however, the large advances invite profit-taking, which causes supply to increase. The effect is that volume peaks, tapers, then leaps again, as selling increases, the market stablizes, and then the uptrend picks up steam again. Somewhere in that activity a gap often occurs because buyers' bids and sellers' offers temporarily fail to match. This gap therefore signals the continuation of the existing trend. (See Figure 4-16.)

FIGURE 4-16 Breakaway, continuation (measuring or runaway), and exhaustion gaps.

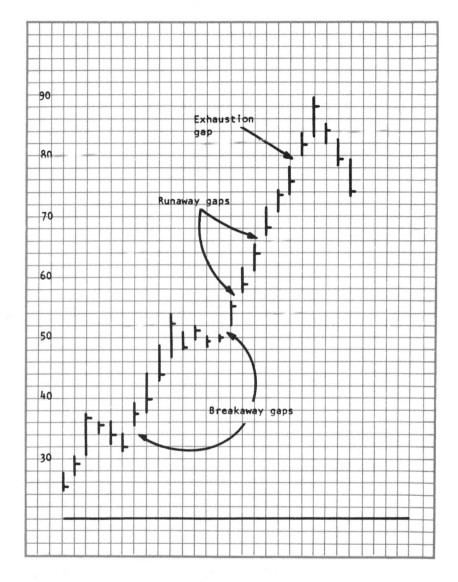

(The same can occur on a decline but not so dramatically. As prices move downward rapidly, selling pressure is temporarily offset by a flurry of demand, again creating the same type of gap.)

A continuation gap is also called a runaway or measuring gap, because it enables the chartist to measure the remaining duration of the trend. These gaps almost invariably appear about half-way through a trend. If you can clearly identify a measuring gap, you have an excellent signal for action. If two or more gaps occur within a trend, the measuring gap is the one during which prices are moving the most fluidly and rapidly.

EXHAUSTION GAP.   True to its name, the exhaustion gap comes at the end of a move; thus its significance is that it signals a reversal. (See Figure 4-16.) To distinguish it from a continuation gap, which signals just the opposite, look for these conditions:

- Volume is high when the gap appears, but it does not taper, as it normally does in a continuation gap. Instead, it drops off sharply.
- The pace of the trend just slows before the gap.
- One or more gaps appear before the one in question. The more preceding (runaway) gaps there are, the more likely the current gap is signalling a reversal.
- The price movement pattern has about run its course anyway. (Price patterns are discussed in detail in Chapters 6 through 8.)

If enough of these conditions come together, you may think in terms of an exhaustion gap. Specifically, look for two things: (1) a reversal (although not ncessarily a major one) on the day after the gap appears and (2) a closing of the gap in two to five days.

Indexes

If you are trading indexes, be aware of the following:

- Common and pattern gaps are rare in index trading.
- Exhaustion and breakaway gaps may occur but only if enough individual issues all have the same or very similar supply and demand conditions prevailing at the same time.

Island Reversals

Island reversals are rare and generally are not detected soon enough to be of any forecasting value. They occur at the turn of a major movement and sometimes within a major movement (such as within a "head and shoulders" pattern, which is explained in detail in later chapters). (See Figure 4-17.)

FIGURE 4-17   An island reversal.

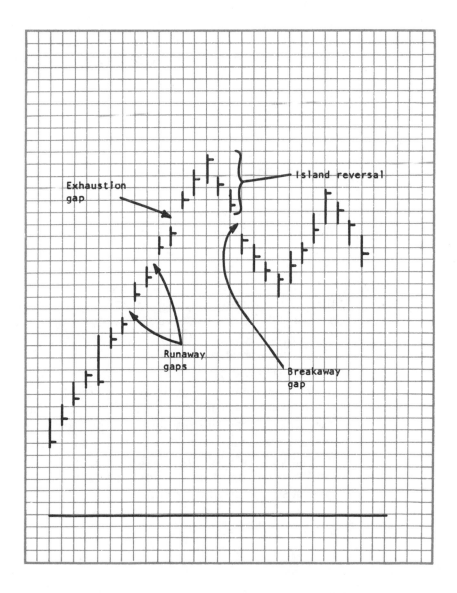

Look for island reversals when the following conditions prevail:

- Prices are moving within a compact trading range, after a long trend.
- An exhaustion gap precedes the reversal and a breakaway gap follows it, both occurring at about the same price levels. (The breakaway may be closed a few days later.)

While island reversals are pretty easy to spot, they are generally clear only by the time they have been completed. As a result, there is little opportunity for profit except by means of some short-term scalping. Long term, however, you may assume that the reversal will stay in effect for a period roughly equivalent to the length of the trend preceding the reversal.

Moving Average (MA)

This analytical tool is much more objective than most at the chartist's disposal. Whereas analysts may disagree as to whether this or that formation is developing, they cannot dispute the precision of a moving average signal.

A moving average is a rolling average of some number of prior prices. For example, a 10-day moving average is calculated by adding up the prior ten days' closing prices, dividing by ten, and plotting the result on the bar chart. (Closing prices are used most often, but sometimes other prices, such as daily midpoints, are also used.) The average is "moving" because this calculation is done daily, each time taking the prior ten days' prices into account. You can do the same for the prior twenty, thirty, forty, or more days. Each time the number of days gets larger, however, the average tracks actual daily prices less and less closely. Compare, for example, the 10- and 40-day moving averages in Figure 4-18. On the other hand, if the moving average is too sensitive, it may give false signals, or "whipsaws."

FIGURE 4-18   Two typical moving averages—10- and 40-day.

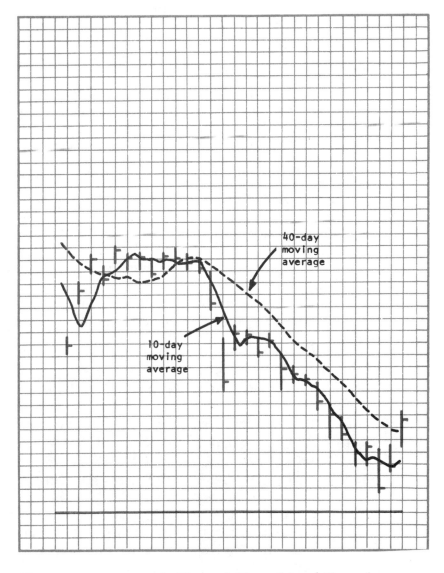

The moving averages in Figure 4-18 are "simple" moving averages, so called because they give equal weight to all the prices in the computation. Some analysts, however, believe that more weight should be assigned to more recent prices.

Accordingly, the linearly weighted moving average assigns multipliers to each of the prices. In a 10-day moving average, the most recent price has a multiplier of 10, the next most recent 9, and so on. Each price is then multiplied by the assigned value. The sum of the weighted prices is divided not by the number of prices (10) but by the total of the multipliers, in this case 55 (10 + 9 + 8 + 7 + 6 + 5 + 4 + 3 + 2 + 1).

An even more sophisticated calculation goes into deriving an exponentially smoothed moving average. The calculation is so complicated, in fact, that it is done only by computer and is available generally only on electronic database chart services.

How Moving Averages Are Used

The value of the moving average is that it can be compared against actual prices, to determine whether a stock, some other security, a futures contract, or a whole market is over- or undervalued. The assumption is that, when prices move beyond the average, they will continue in that direction for a while. A price movement above the average is a buy signal; one below the average, a sell signal.

FILTERS.   The worth of the buy and sell signals, however, can be reduced by a too-sensitive moving average. To avoid "whipsaws," you can use "filters," such as:

- Besides requiring the closing (or midpoint) prices to clear the moving average, you might wait until the entire day's trading range clears.
- You might hold out until prices clear the moving average by a certain percentage, such as 10% of the stock's value. But be careful. Too low a percentage and the penetration may not really be signaling a trend. Too high a percentage and maybe the signal will come too late to do much about it.

Related to this requirement are percentage envelopes, or volatility bands. If you are plotting a moving average on a computer, you might program the system to plot two lines parallel to the moving average. One would be a certain percentage above and the other the same percentage below it. Price penetrations beyond this envelope, or beyond these bands, would then constitute signals. (See Figure 4-18.)

In a double crossover, a buy signal is generated when the shorter average crosses above the longer one, a sell signal when it crosses below the longer-term average. The rationale is that the longer average lags the market a bit more than the shorter-term one, so that a crossover is less likely to result in a whipsaw.

Two averages can also be used as a kind of buffer zone, the requirement being that prices must penetrate above both averages before you take action.

A triple crossover usually involves 4-, 9-, and 18-day moving averages. In an uptrend, the logical configuration would have the 4-day MA (the most sensitive) below the less sensitive 9-day MA, which is below the least sensitive 18-day MA. When the 4-day average moves above the two others, you have a fairly strong buy signal; short-term prices are moving well above long-term averages. The reverse is true in a downtrend: When the 4-day moves below the others, you have a pretty clear sell signal; short-term prices are under the long-term averages. In either type of trend, some intermingling can and does occur, but the order generally remains intact.

Relative Strength Index (RSI)

The term "relative" normally implies a comparison of one entity with another. In technical analysis, relative strength is the comparison of some period's average of up closes to the same period's average of down closes. (For purposes of this discussion, an up-close is a closing price higher than the prior day's close; a down-close is lower than the previous day's.) For example, suppose you wanted to calculate the relative strength of one month's (20 trading days') worth of price activity. Those 20 closing prices are as follows (the first price is assumed to be an up close):

Day	Price	Day	Price	Day	Price
1	20u	8	22-1/8u	15	25u
2	20-1/8u	9	22d	16	25-1/4u
3	20d	10	22-1/8u	17	25-1/8d
4	19-3/4d	11	22-3/8u	18	25d
5	19-5/8d	12	23-1/4u	19	24-7/8d
6	19-3/4u	13	23-5/8u	20	24-3/4d
7	20u	14	24-1/4u		

Remembering that each ⅛-point is equal to $.125, the sum of all up closes is 267⅞ (267.875), and the sum of all downcloses is 181⅛ (181.125). There are 12 upcloses and 8 downcloses. The average upclose value is 22.32 (267.875 divided by 12), the average downclose 22.64 (181.125 divided by 8). These values are then compared in the following formula:

$$RS = \frac{\text{Average upclose value}}{\text{Average downclose value}}$$

$$= \frac{22.32}{22.64} = .9589$$

The relative strength, by itself, does not tell you much. The value is generally incorporated into another formula that gives us the relative strength index, an indicator that was developed by J. Welles Wilder, Jr. The RSI formula is as follows:

$$RSI = 100 - \frac{100}{100 + RS}$$

$$= 100 - \frac{100}{1 + .9859}$$

$$= 49.65$$

How do you use this value? RSI is plotted on a vertical scale of 0 to 100. When prices are up above the 70 level (80 in bull markets), the instrument is considered overbought. When it is under 30 (20 in bear markets), it is undersold.

Failure swings occur at the high and low ends of the RSI scale. A bottom failure swing occurs when, in a downtrend, the RSI fails to set a new low and then goes on to set a new high. This is sometimes a buy signal. (See Figure 4-19.) A top failure swing is the result when, in an uptrend, the RSI fails to set a new high and then goes on to a new low. Watch for the signal to sell. (See Figure 4-20.)

A word of caution about RSI: Extreme price movements are bound to create similar movement in the RSI. Taking action on the basis of a single move into an overbought or undersold area can often be premature. The point is not to jump into or out of a position just on the basis of the RSI indicator. Usually the first move into the extreme zone is a warning; even the second move could be a false signal. Use RSI as it is intended to be—an indicator. And use it only in connection with everything else you see in price movement, volume, and the like.

FIGURE 4-19 A bottom failure swing. Note how, at B, the RSI fails to exceed a previous trough, A, and then goes on to set a new high, C.

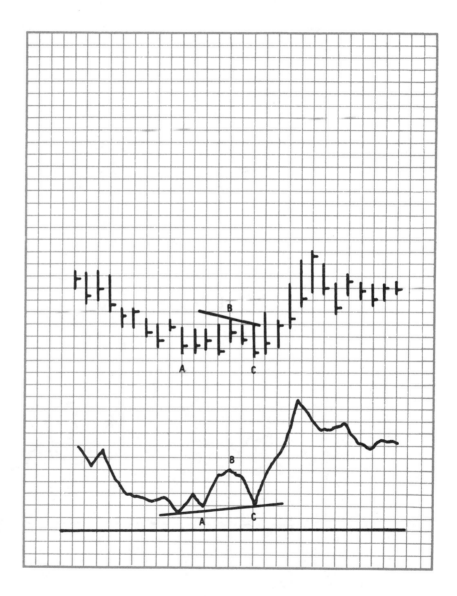

FIGURE 4-20   A top failure swing. At B, the RSI fails to set a new high (compared with A), and then goes on to set a new low, C.

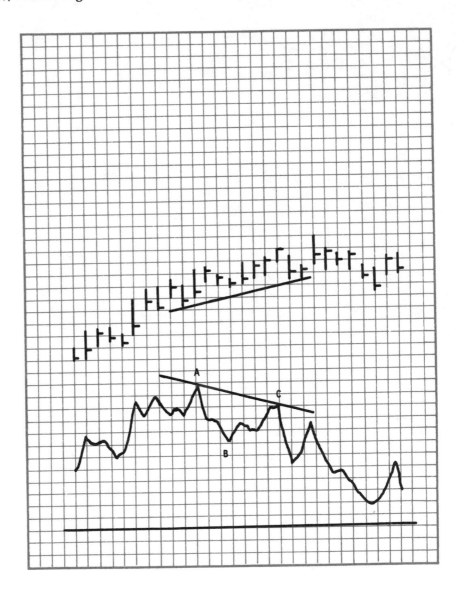

Confirmation and Divergence

This last point regarding RSI applies to technical analysis in general. Never act on the basis of one signal. Always look for confirmation of a trend or reversal. If price action is telling you one thing, look at volume, the moving averages, support and resistance, and the overall pattern. Also weigh whatever information you have— whether it derives from charting or anywhere else. For example, if all the technical indicators tell you that corn prices are about to go down, don't ignore the headlines in the financial news about the corn blight in the Midwest.

In other words, always look for confirmation or divergence among the indicators. To take our example a step farther, an imminent corn blight is a diverging indicator; it heralds scarcities and rising prices, even though everything on the charts indicates a downturn. If a bumper crop were in the offing, then the news would act as a confirming indicator; prices are now very likely to go down.

Even among the technical indicators, these principles apply. For example, suppose prices are moving upward steadily, but on diminishing volume. Prices are indicating an uptrend—and so you would draw the trendline—but volume is telling you that the interest among market participants is simply not there. In fact, fewer and fewer are staying in the market. Volume is therefore said diverge from prices; it indicates that the uptrend is not a strong one and that it probably will not last long or go far.

Any chartist will tell you: Never forget the principles of confirmation and divergence.

Trendlines, channels, support, resistance, gaps, moving averages, relative strength index—these are the building blocks of technical analysis. The next step is to put these building blocks together, so as to determine when they are confirming one another and when they are diverging. The most coherent way of going about this task is to describe the phases of price movement, the various patterns that characterize each phase, and the behavior of each of these indicators within a pattern. This is what we cover in Chapters 5-8.

5
Accumulation

Prices can move through four major phases of price movement:

- In the accumulation phase, supply and demand compete for
  dominance, but as time goes by buyers slowly edge out sellers.
  Prices creep upward, and knowledgeable longs take more and
  more stock off the market, in anticipation of increasing prices.
  This period frequently follows a major decline in prices and
  spans at least six months, during which a bottom is established
  for a sustained uptrend in prices. Consequently, the patterns
  appearing in this phase are classified as major reversal patterns.
  By the completion of the accumulation phase, large portions of
  the stock have been taken off the market and held by staunch
  longs, who are willing to wait for their price. The stock is now
  ready for a sizable and prolonged advance.

    This phase occurs only in securities markets, not in futures
  markets, where the supply of contracts is unlimited.

- The markup phase, a major trend, begins with the breakout, in
  which prices penetrate resistance and which is often led by a
  breakaway gap on heavy volume. Buyers are becoming more
  aggressive, bidding higher. Eventually prices turn upward. During this phase, prices sometimes hesitate but then continue upward. The resultant movements are therefore known as con-

tinuation patterns. Traditionally, volume is heavier on advances, lighter on retracements. Relative strength, however, continues on a generally upward slope, slacking off only when continuation patterns are in the making.

• Toward the end of the major trend is the distribution phase, during which selling begins to dominate prices and the stock moves to more willing holders. Prices are getting ready to move downward. During this phase, the price movement hesitations are considered reversal patterns, just as in the accumulation phase. Their configurations, however, are "flipped," so that peaks become troughs and vice versa.

• The markdown phase starts once support is violated during distribution. Readily available supply outweighs demand, as prices drop, often creating a breakaway gap. Volume dries up whenever prices attempt to advance in what are sometimes called "rigor mortis rallies." Volume does not, however, have to expand when prices move downward; you can be in a markdown phase without heavy volume accompanying the declines. Relative strength remains on a steady downward slope, easing off only during the moments of hesitation. Continuation patterns develop during this decline, as they do in the markup phase, but they are also "flipped."

This chapter presents the reversal patterns found in the accumulation phase. Subsequent chapters will cover the other three phases. In all cases, the patterns will be described in terms of price action, volume, support/resistance, moving average, relative strength, and forecasting value. The terminology will be brief and to the point.

Note: Not all patterns will be drawn "to scale." That is, in reality a pattern may require months to develop—which would translate into many sheets of graph paper. To keep the presentation simple and manageable, each pattern will be confined to one "sheet" with the duration noted below the time scale.

From time to time, allusions will be made to the underlying psychology of the market participants in the patterns presented. Explaining the psychology in each and every case, however, would require a volume of its own. Over the course of the chapters on patterns, think always about underlying motivations and reactions of the buyers and sellers. Ask yourself why prices are acting as they are, why volume is trending up or down, why the moving average or relative strength would behave in one fashion or another. A grasp on the psychology of the market is worth far more than simply memorizing the characteristics of patterns.

In the following accumulation patterns, keep two things in mind about gaps. First, common and ex-dividend gaps are almost invariably meaningless from a technical point of view. Second, a breakaway gap (when it appears) at the point that prices penetrate resistance is a good indication that the markup phase, with its long-term advance in prices is coming. Similarly, a breakaway gap following a prolonged distribution is usually a reliable signal that the markdown has begun.

Rectangular Base Pattern (Neutral or Flat Bottom)

Price Action

In this simple, easily identifiable pattern, highs and lows alternate within a tight trading range (see Figure 5-1). Taking up to six months to develop, the major (or at least intermediate) trend is neutral, with minor up- and downtrends.

Volume

Heavy volume early in the pattern tapers off as prices zig-zag. Heavy volume during price declines and the occasional spurt of volume during advances usually indicate distribution; holders are selling off. As prices creep upward, volume increases, eventually becoming synchronized with price direction and indicating a strong test of resistance with a possible breakout.

Support/Resistance

Major support runs clearly along the bottom of the trading range, major resistance along the top.

FIGURE 5-1   A rectangular base pattern (neutral or flat bottom).

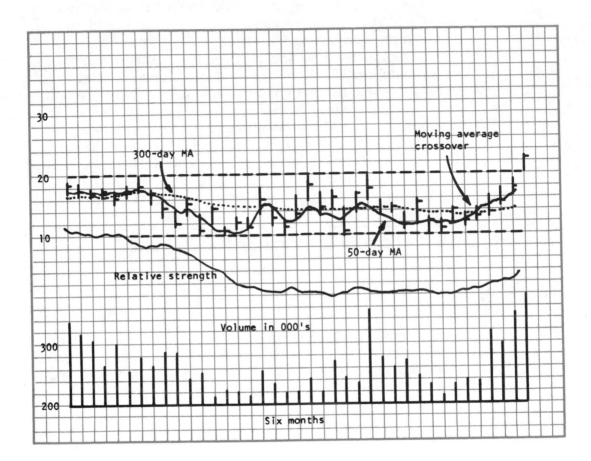

Moving Averages

Whipsaws in the MAs can fool you. Wait for the 50-day MA to cross over and above the 200-day MA—a sign of an impending breakout.

Relative Strength

Since the pattern takes so long to develop, RS tends to track price action fairly closely. Its gradual upturn toward the end of the configuration is an indicator that prices may be ready to break out.

Forecasting Value

Once you have determined that prices have broken out (taking all the indicators into account), you can estimate the minimum duration of the uptrend. Simply take the height of the rectangle and add it to the breakout point. In Figure 5-1, the height of the pattern is 10 points (from 10 to 20). Add 10 to the breakout point at the 20 level, and you can forecast at least a 10-point advance in prices to the 30.

Exercise

In Figure 5-1:

- Draw and label lines indicating support and resistance levels.
- Identify a breakout point and list at least two indicators of the breakout.
- Estimate the minimum level of advance in prices.

Compare your chart with Figure 5-2.

FIGURE 5-2   Answer to exercise.

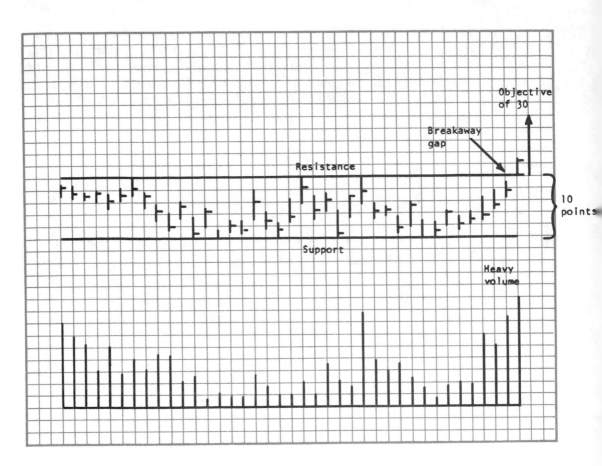

Duplex Horizontal Pattern
(Step-Up or Step-Down Bottom)

Sometimes one rectangular pattern follows another. The trading range of the second rectangle, however, is slightly higher or lower than that of the first. Hence the names "step-up" and "step-down." Instead of the expected major advance following the first formation, prices simply go on to another rectangle. In the long run, the advance, when it comes, will be greater because of the prolonged bottom activity. Simply apply what you know about rectangular patterns to the second formation.

Saucer Pattern (Rounding Bottom)

Price Action

Buying pressure slowly overcomes selling in a pattern that can take at least several months and often a full year to evolve. The result is a prolonged, curving configuration whose trend is neutral. (See Figure 5-3.)

FIGURE 5-3   Saucer pattern (rounding bottom).

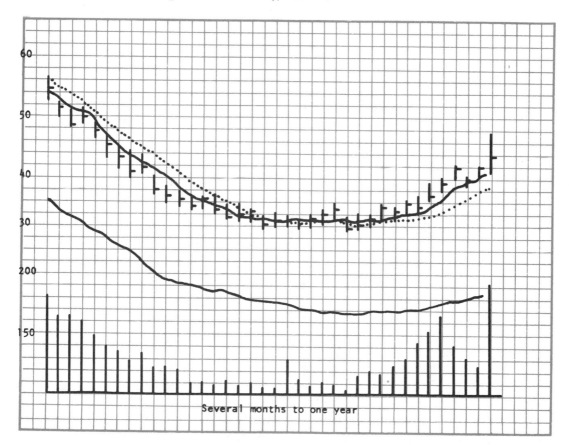

Volume

Generally interest tracks prices, slacking off toward the middle of the pattern and picking up toward the end. If the saucer forms a "handle" or "tail," volume is likely to drop off again.

Support/Resistance

At the middle of the pattern in Figure 5-3, prices frequently test the 30 level without breaking through. Major support is thus identified at the 30 level. Resistance is found at the top of the handle; in fact it causes the saucer to flatten out to form the handle.

Moving Averages

Watch for the 50-day MA to cross over the 200-day MA.

Relative Strength

There is no typical pattern. RS may turn down or remain neutral due to the stock's general inactivity. As the stock moves upward, RS will at least flatten out and perhaps even turn upward itself.

Forecasting Value

To forecast a minimum price level (or "objective"), take the distance between the highest and lowest points in the saucer, and add that distance to the breakout point. The calculation itself is easy. What is slightly harder is identifying where precisely the saucer begins and ends.

Exercise

In Figure 5-3:

- Outline the saucer and handle, identifying the beginning and end points of the overall pattern.
- Draw the lines for support and resistance.
- Calculate the minimum extent of the upside advance.

Compare your chart with the one in Figure 5-4 (on p. 114).

Dormant Bottom

Price Action

In a pattern that lives up to its name, prices move in a distinctly neutral trend. (See Figure 5-5.) The action is peppered with meaningless gaps—signs only of the lack of interest in the issue. Finally, after a period that can last for years, prices break sharply in an upward curving trend.

FIGURE 5-5 Dormant bottom.

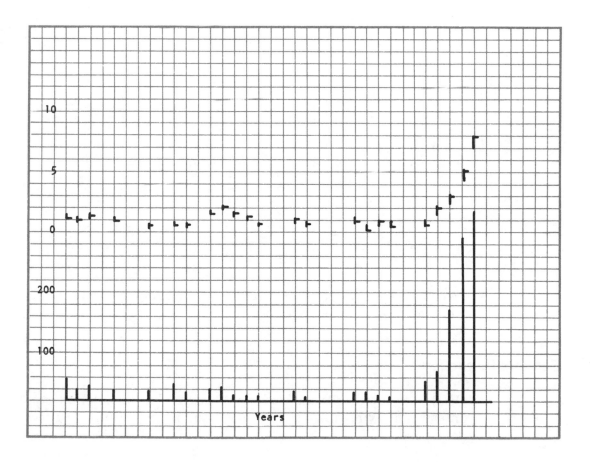

FIGURE 5-4   Answer to exercise.

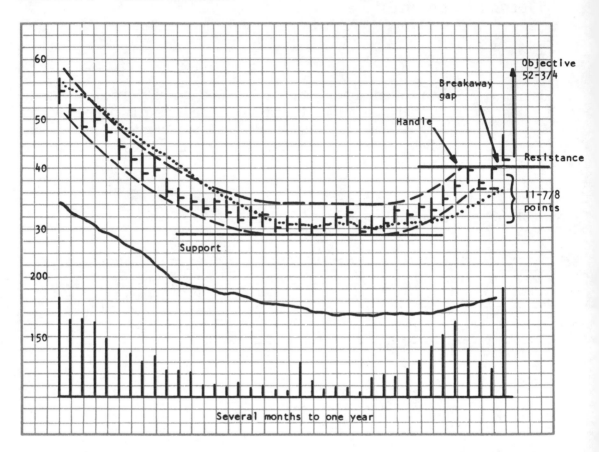

Volume

Volume is negligible throughout the pattern, exploding only at the very end when prices jump upward.

Support/Resistance

These levels are difficult and often impossible to detect. Any attempts at laying down lines would result in largely "imaginary" levels.

Moving Averages

MAs are rendered all but meaningless since the stock often will not even trade every day.

Relative Strength

Trying to interpret RS is futile. The stock is either too inactive (most of the time) or too volatile (toward the end of the pattern).

Forecasting Value

Wait for prices to move. Only then do you have a chance at meaningful charting.

Head and Shoulders Bottom
(Inverted Head and Shoulders)

Price Action

Picture the pattern in Figure 5-6 upside down, and you will see why it is called a "head and shoulders." Prices test the 34-35 level twice, each peak part of a "shoulder" in the pattern. Between the two shoulders is a test of the 25 level—the "head." Connecting the shoulders is the "neckline"—in this case the 34-35-point level—which is not always perfectly horizontal. This configuration, a major neutral trend, can take three to six months to develop.

Volume

The left shoulder sees the lightest volume, but interest tracks upward as the pattern unfolds. By the time the right shoulder is completed, volume is at its heaviest.

FIGURE 5-6   Head and shoulders bottom (inverted head and shoulders).

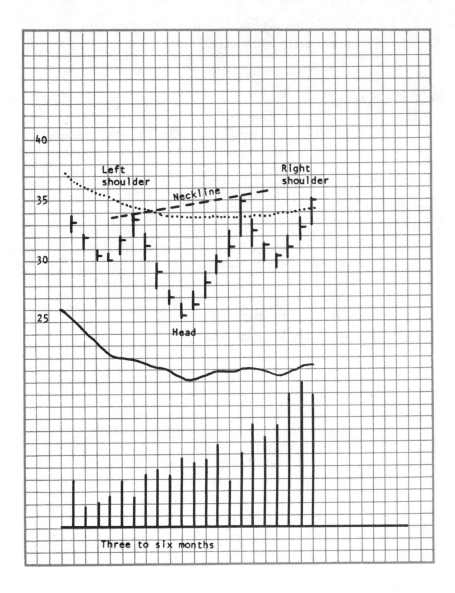

Support/Resistance

Support is considered major at the extremity of the head, minor at the shoulder levels. Major resistance is found at the neckline, which is broken when prices start moving upward.

Moving Averages

Prices may whipsaw across both MAs, giving off false signals if you do not recognize the pattern. The crossover of the 50-day MA over the 200-day MA is a sign, however, that the breakout is coming.

Relative Strength

RS remains flat throughout most of the pattern, turning upward slightly as prices break out.

Forecasting Value

Measure the vertical distance from the neckline to the bottom of the head. Add that distance to the breakout point for a minimum price advance.

Exercise

In Figure 5-6:

• Draw and label support and resistance levels.
• Calculate a price objective.

Compare your responses with Figure 5-7.

FIGURE 5-7   Answer to exercise.

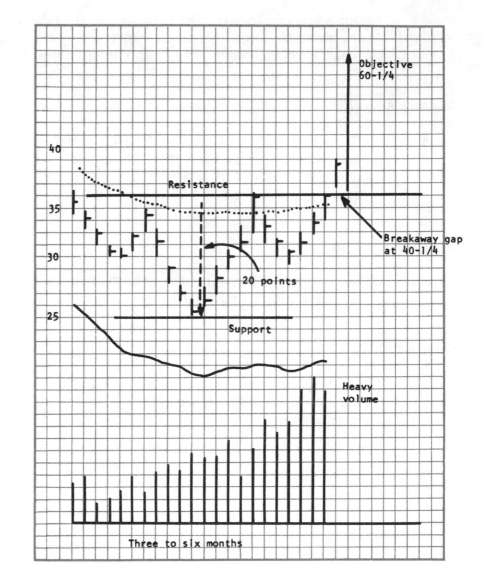

V Bottom (Spike Reversal)

Price Action

This short pattern takes only days to happen, although it can be part of a months-long major bottom. (See Figure 5-8.) Amid great volatility, a steady downtrend in prices deteriorates into a cascade, which is both created by and causes much short selling. Runaway gaps and finally an exhaustion gap may occur. The turnaround comes on the key reversal day, which is often so hard to detect that you probably will not see it until it is long over. From this point, the uptrend builds.

Sometimes the V pattern tapers off into a handle. (See Figure 5-9). This is a tight trading range in which buyers are going long in a more orderly way than during the V itself. The tail can extend the V pattern for some time, but certainly no longer than six months. (The combination of the V and the tail gives rise to the sometimes used name of "square root pattern.")

Volume

Volume escalates as prices fall, demonstrating great participation by sellers. Peak volume and the lowest point of the V coincide on the key reversal day. If a handle forms, volume tapers off, generally surging as prices advance in minor trends.

Support/Resistance

Neither support nor resistance is discernible during the V pattern itself. You have to go back over the stock's prior activity to look for these levels. Upon completion of the V, however, major support can be assumed at the key reversal day level; this support becomes stronger as prices test it during the handle (if any). The longer the handle persists, however, the closer support gets to the bottom of the handle.

Resistance may be evident historically well above the handle, but it draws down closer to the top of the handle as time goes by.

FIGURE 5-8   V bottom (spike reversal).

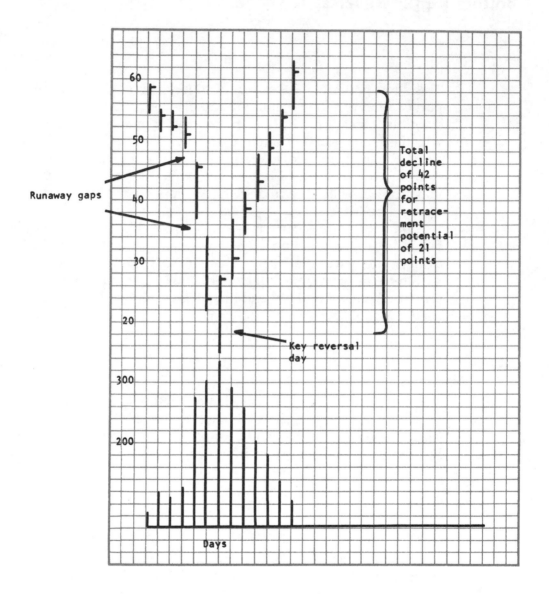

FIGURE 5-9   V bottom with handle.

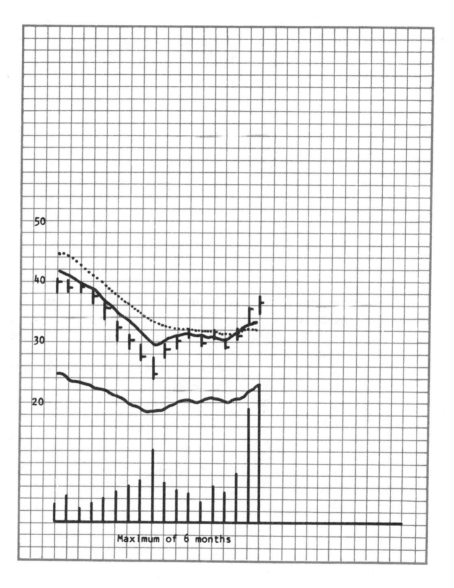

Moving Averages

Prices of course drop well below both averages, making at least a "technical correction" likely. As prices return to the general area of the averages, look for the 50-day MA to cross over the 200-day average.

Relative Strength

RS is largely neutral throughout this formation.

Forecasting Value

Short term, you can look for at least a 50% retracement of the sharp decline. In Figure 5-8, the total loss amounts to 45 points, from 60 down to 15. If you can identify the key reversal day quickly enough, you might be able to participate in the retracement of 22½ points or so.

Beyond the day trader's point of view, look for the breakout point—ideally a breakaway gap—in the handle, accompanied by heavy volume. At that point measure the perpendicular distance from the top of the handle to the key reversal day in the V pattern. Add that distance to the breakout point for a minimum price advance.

Exercise

In Figure 5-9:

- Draw the lines of major support and resistance, if any.
- Identify the price levels of the key reversal day, the top of the handle, and the breakout point.
- Calculate the minimum price objective.

   Compare your responses with the chart in Figure 5-10.

FIGURE 5-10   Answer to exercise.

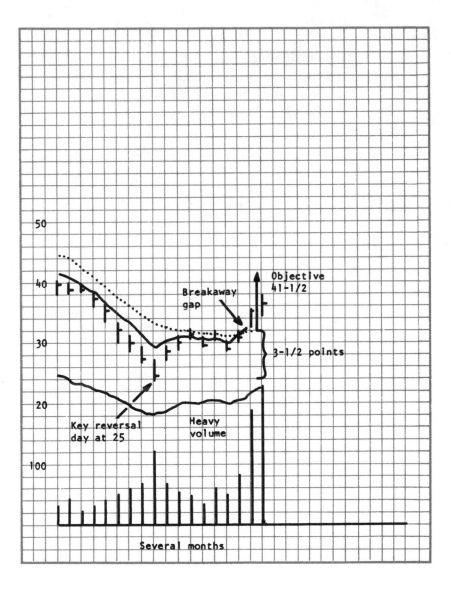

Double Bottom (W Pattern)

Price Action

When prices test support more than once, they can form a W pattern. (See Figure 5-11.) This is a V pattern, followed by at least a 15% retracement, and then a second test. The trends must all be considered minor, up or down, until prices eventually break out over the level of the middle peak. At that point, you might be thinking in terms of a long-term uptrend. The two lows may be separated in time by a month or more, with the whole configuration taking three to four months to be completed. This pattern may pertain to either an individual stock or an index.

Volume

The first trough is accompanied by heavy volume, which then diminishes as the pattern unfolds. This drying up of volume indicates that buyers are accumulating the stock and holding it.

Support/Resistance

Major support can be found along the line of the two troughs.

After the first decline, prices advance because the stock is generally oversold and traders are looking for bargains. But resistance develops at the middle peak, as the same bargain hunters take profits and long-term holders of the stock see an opportunity to cut their losses. Hence prices decline again. After the second trough, prices may encounter some resistance at the same level, but it will not be strong.

Moving Averages

Be wary if the 50-day average moves over the 200-day MA at or about the middle peak. If the pattern is indeed a W, this is a false signal. If prices dip far enough below the 50-day average during the second trough, however, you might look for some rebound effect.

FIGURE 5-11   Double bottom (W pattern).

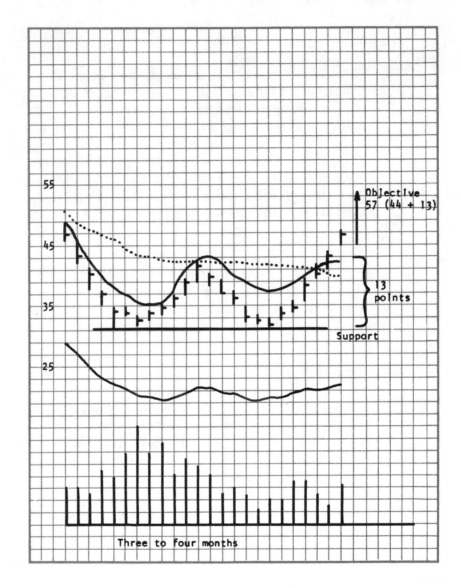

Relative Strength

The stock may seem like a poor performer if relative strength goes to a lower low during the second trough. But many worthwhile stocks have bottomed out on poor relative strength before going on to a great advance.

Forecasting Value

To compute a minimum price advance, take the vertical distance between the high and low points of the W pattern, and add it to the breakout point. In Figure 5-11, that distance is 13 points added to the breakout point of 44, for an objective of 57.

Triple Bottom (Sawtooth) Pattern

Price Action

Before you go off and buy the stock in Figure 5-11, however, you want to be certain that it is not in the middle of a triple bottom, or sawtooth, configuration. If so, prices will eventually break out, but you might have to wait up to six months to take your profits. Compare the first two peaks, with the middle trough, in Figure 5-12 with those in Figure 5-11. In the sawtooth pattern, prices are not able to break upward on the second advance.

Volume

Volume is the same as in the W pattern, but it tapers off after the second peak.

Support/Resistance

Support is strong, having exerted itself through three break-through attempts. Should prices decline in the future, this support is likely to hold again.

Resistance is equally evident but not as strong as support. Prices eventually will break upward.

Moving Averages

Watch for whipsaws as the 50-day MA crosses the longer-term average again on the second peak. This will happen in a prolonged bottom movement.

FIGURE 5-12   Triple bottom (sawtooth) pattern.

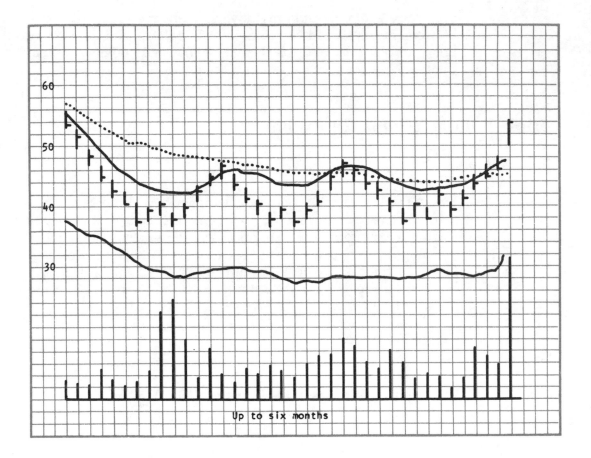

Relative Strength

RS bottoms with price at the two troughs, bending slowly upward toward the end of the formation.

Forecasting Value

A price objective is calculated in the same way as in the W pattern.

Exercise

In Figure 5-12:

- Identify major support and resistance.
- Mark the breakout point.
- Calculate the price objective.

Compare your responses with the chart in Figure 5-13.

FIGURE 5-13   Answer to exercise.

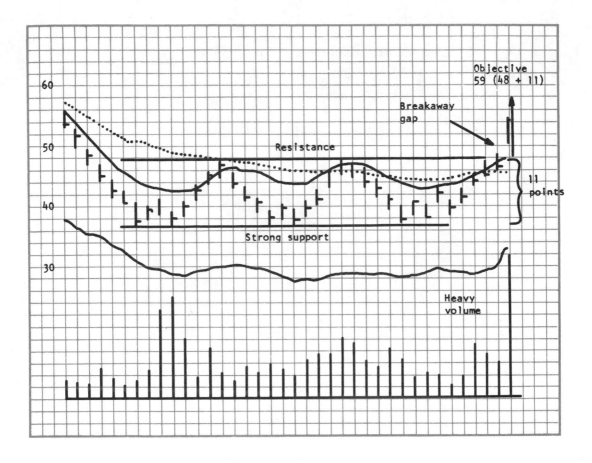

Island Reversal

Price Action

Coming at the end of a "waterfall" in prices, the island reversal differs from the V bottom in that it curves into a U shape and takes a little longer—days instead of one day—to unwind. (See Figure 5-14.) The minor trends are steeply down and then just as sharply upward, with a few days of rounding prices between the down- and upslopes. The pattern is called an "island" because the in-between price activity is cut off by measuring (or runaway) gaps and an exhaustion gap on the downtrend, and by a breakaway gap on the uptrend.

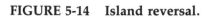

FIGURE 5-14   Island reversal.

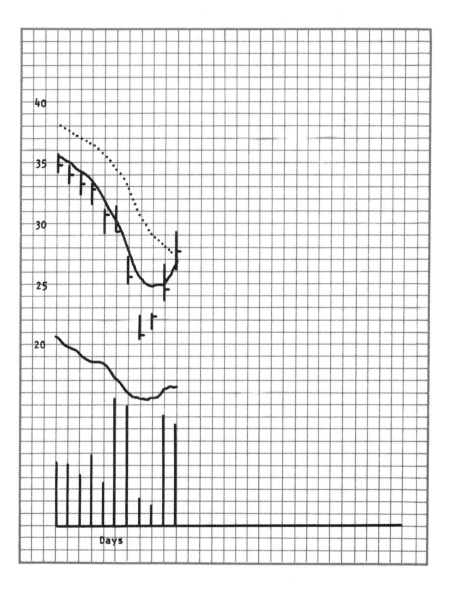

Volume

The cascade in prices occurs on heavy volume, which dries up during the rebound. Eventually volume explodes as the breakout occurs, sometime after this pattern runs its course.

Support/Resistance

The reversal point indicates strong support. Resistance is very hard to discern, if it is there at all.

Moving Averages

Moving averages are of little use during the precipitous drop in prices. The percentage of difference between prices and the averages, however, indicates the degree that the stock is oversold.

Relative Strength

RS tracks price activity, forming a U and eventually turning upwards upon the breakout.

Forecasting Value

There is very little time for accumulation during an island reversal, so there is little information on which to calculate an objective. A general rule of thumb, however, is that you can look for at least a 50% retracement of the minor downtrend.

Exercise

In Figure 5-14:

- Identify the runaway (measuring) gaps, exhaustion gap, and breakaway gap.
- Circle the island reversal.
- Identify the height of the pattern and the percentage of retracement.

Compare your results with the chart in Figure 5-15.

FIGURE 5-15   Answer to exercise.

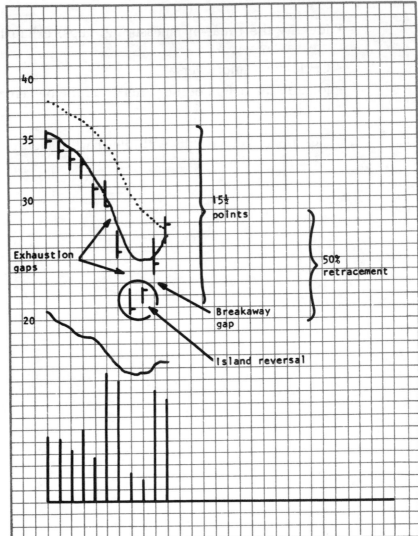

Throughout the patterns in the accumulation phase, buying pressure has been building. Prices have been "accumulating" demand. Now they are ready to break out upwards.

6

The Markup Phase

Ideally, the accumulation phase ends with a breakout in prices, accompanied by heavy volume. This is the beginning of the markup phase, during which prices advance over the long term. Aggressive buyers, entering the market in force, create constantly higher highs and lows—an unmistakble uptrend. The only question is where the market turns. Getting into the market early in the markup is easier than knowing when to get out, taking as much profit with you as possible. The patterns described in this chapter will help you in making that sell decision.

Note: As in the accumulation phase, the occurrence of common and ex-dividend gaps is not meaningful.

Falling Flag

Price Action

Early in the markup phase, prices may advance sharply, forming a "pole," then retrace in a small channel of minor up- and down-trends, which resembles a flag. (See Figure 6-1.) While the pole may form in a few days, the flag can take another week or so, for a total formation time of about two weeks. If the pattern lasts longer than two weeks, the breakout might be considered a false start.

FIGURE 6-1 Falling flag.

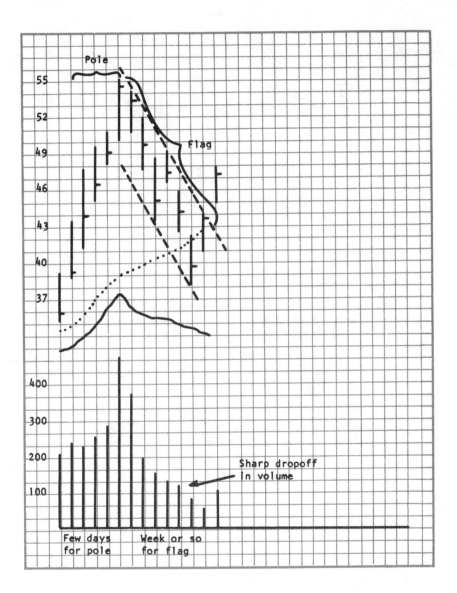

Volume

Interest mounts quickly during the formation of the pole, but then it drops off as the flag unfurls. When the upside trend resumes, this time presumably for the long term, volume picks up again.

Support/Resistance

Look for support and resistance in the previous bottom formation. If the flag has already penetrated previous resistance, then there is no way of calculating where it might be.

Moving Averages

These play a small part because the formation is so brief and volatile. The pole may extend well above the 200-day MA, but this is not a sign of anything meaningful.

Relative Strength

RS will not drop as much as the stock itself. Yet, given the rapidity of the formation, RS is of little value.

Forecasting Value

In the short run, you may look for the flag channel to retrace about 50% of the pole. Beyond that, once you are satisfied that prices are in a long-term upward trend, add the height of the pole to the breakout point, and calculate the price objective from the top of the pole.

Exercise

In Figure 6-1:

- Measure the height of the pole.
- Calculate a price objective if the breakout were to occur immediately after the flag.

Compare your results with Figure 6-2.

FIGURE 6-2 Answer to exercise.

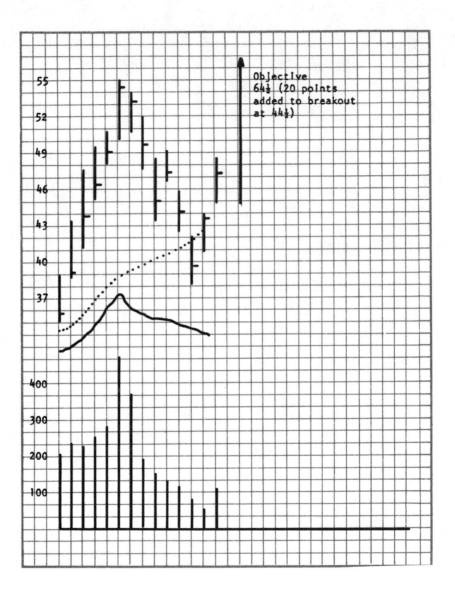

Pennant

Compared to the flag, the pennant has the same characteristics with respect to volume, support, resistance, moving averages, relative strength, and forecasting value. It differs only in terms of price action. (See Figure 6-3.) At times, a pennant will form after a flag; that is, a pole will form at the end of the flag's channel, from which the pennant then develops.

FIGURE 6-3   Pennant.

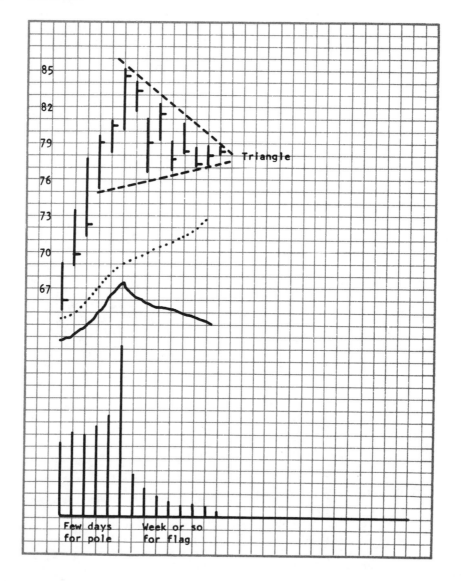

Price Action

This pattern is the same as the flag, except that prices taper off into an increasingly tighter trading range characterized by lower highs and higher lows. Also like the flag, the pennant should be complete within days. The longer it takes to develop fully, the more suspicious you might be as to whether the breakout has really occurred.

2</

Exercise

In Figure 6-4:

- Draw the trend and channel lines that define the flag and pennant.
- Assuming a long-term trend follows the pennant, calculate a minimum price objective.

Compare your results with the chart in Figure 6-5.

FIGURE 6-4 Pennant in exercise.

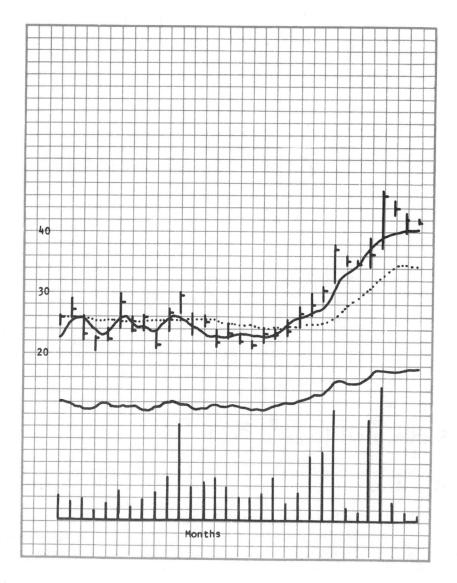

FIGURE 6-5   Answer to exercise.

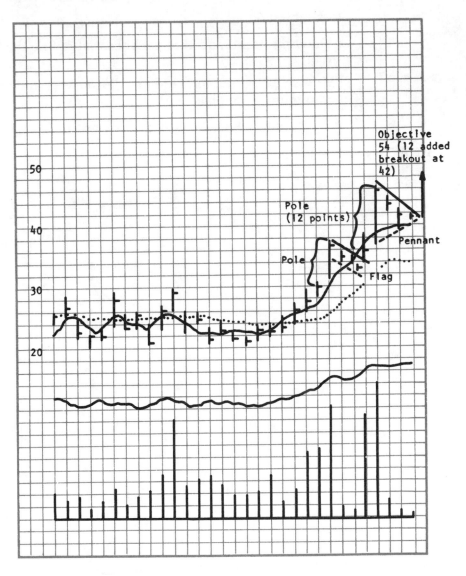

Symmetrical Triangle (Coil)

Price Action

Sometimes a pennant-like formation, called a symmetrical triangle or coil, can develop over a period that may be as short as several weeks or as long as several months. (See Figure 6-6.) The pattern differs from the pennant in that there is no preceding sharp up-swing in prices—that is, no "pole." The coil is regarded as a consolidation (rather than a continuation) pattern because of its tight trading pattern, with lower highs and higher lows. This is a largely unpredictable pattern because prices can break out in either direction; buyers and sellers are about equal in strength. Although the coil often occurs during a major uptrend, the trend during the formation of the pattern—minor or intermediate—can only be described as neutral.

FIGURE 6-6   Symmetrical triangle (coil).

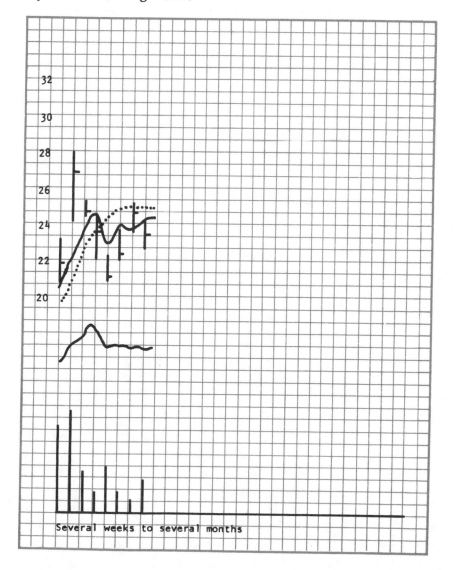

Volume

As in the pennant, volume starts out heavy and then tapers off, with an occasional meaningless burst. It may be expected to pick up when prices break out of either side of the coil, but beware—the pattern is so unreliable that the "breakout" could be a whipsaw.

Support/Resistance

A series of support levels can be found at the successively higher lows, but these are not significant. The same can be said for the resistance levels at the higher highs.

Moving Averages

The 200-day MA will flatten out and occasionally be penetrated by prices and by the 50-day average. When prices cross above the longer average about three-quarters of the way through the pattern, you can start looking for a major uptrend.

Relative Strength

RS moves sideways or perhaps turns downward slightly.

Forecasting Value

When you identify a breakout in either direction, you can calculate a price objecive. For an upswing, add the height of the coil at its widest point to the breakout point. For a downturn, deduct it from the breakout.

Exercise

In Figure 6-7:

- Draw lines identifying the symmetrical triangle.
- Identify the breakout point.
- Calculate the price objective.

    Compare your results with Figure 6-8.

FIGURE 6-7   **Symmetrical triangle (coil) for exercise.**

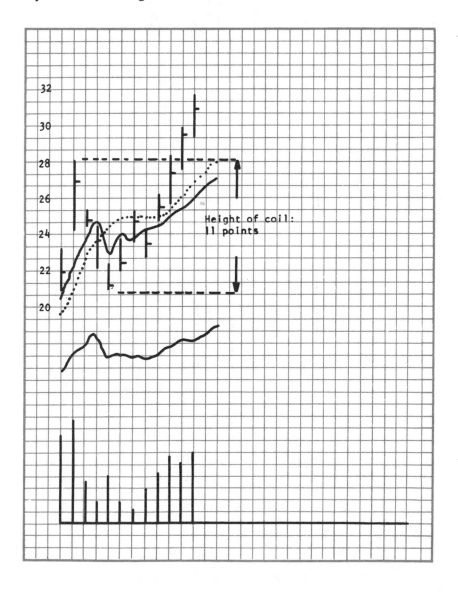

FIGURE 6-8   **Answer to exercise.**

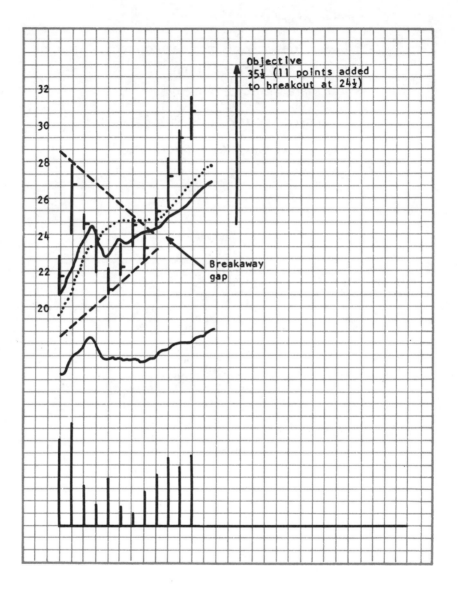

Ascending Triangle

Price Action

For a short while—typically four to six weeks—prices stop advancing; some holders want to take their profits. Nevertheless, buyers are entering the market. The result is fairly constant highs with ever higher lows. (See Figure 6-9.) This period of price consolidation renders the long-term uptrend neutral for all practical purposes.

Volume

Heavy at the outset, volume tends to shrivel as the pattern forms.

Support/Resistance

Support can be expected at the lowest low in the formation. Much more visible is the line of resistance at the top of the triangle.

Moving Averages

Prices may cross the 50-day average more than once without meaning. When they touch the 200-day MA, however, you may look for a buying opportunity.

Relative Strength

There is nothing of significance in the RS indicator.

Forecasting Value

For a minimum upside objective, add the height of the triangle at its widest part to the level of resistance.

FIGURE 6-9   Ascending triangle.

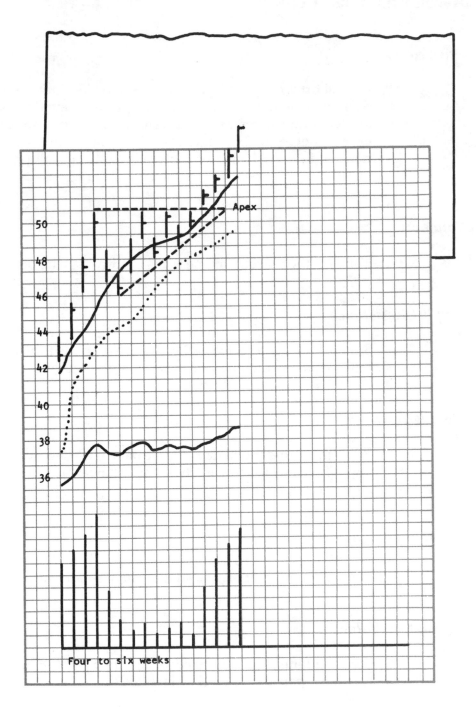

Exercise

In Figure 6-9:

- Draw lines representing support and resistance.
- Measure the height of the triangle.
- Identify the breakaway point.
- Calculate the minimum upside price objective.

Compare your results with Figure 6-10.

FIGURE 6-10   Answer to exercise.

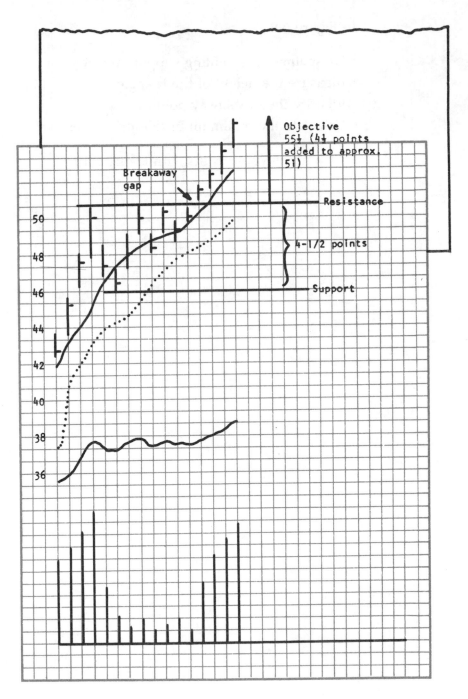

Continuation Head and Shoulders

Price Action

Although the head and shoulders pattern is normally considered a reversal pattern, occurring at the turns of major trends, it may also act as a consolidation or continuation formation. (See Figure 6-11.) Price action, unfolding over the course of several months, is the same described in the last chapter, but the intermediate trend is neutral.

Volume

In the continuation version of the head and shoulders pattern, volume follows no pattern—unlike the distinct pattern in the reversal.

Support/Resistance

Minor support is detectable at the lower points of the shoulders, major support at the tip of the head. Resistance is fairly clear along the neckline.

Moving Averages

Prices and both averages may cross more than once, all of it without much meaning. Count on whipsaws.

Relative Strength

RS tails off into a slow downturn. When prices break upward again, it too resumes its upward direction.

Forecasting Value

Take the distance from the neckline to the tip of the head, and add it to the breakout point.

FIGURE 6-11 Continuation head and shoulders.

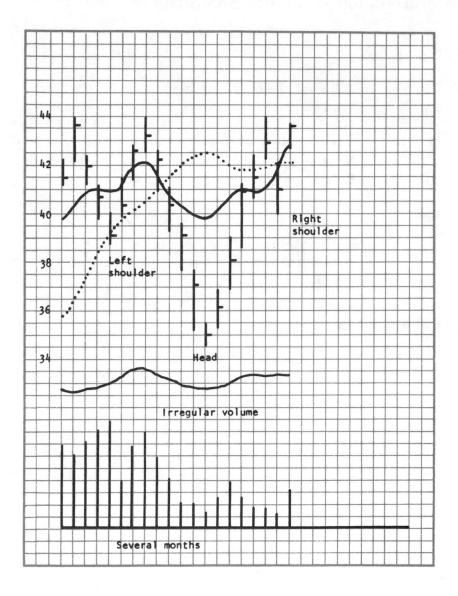

Exercise

In Figure 6-12:

- Draw the trendlines defining the head and shoulders pattern.
- Identify the minor and major support levels, as well as the level of major resistance.
- Locate the breakout point.
- Calculate an upside objective.

  Compare your responses with those in Figure 6-13.

FIGURE 6-12 Continuation head and shoulders for exercise.

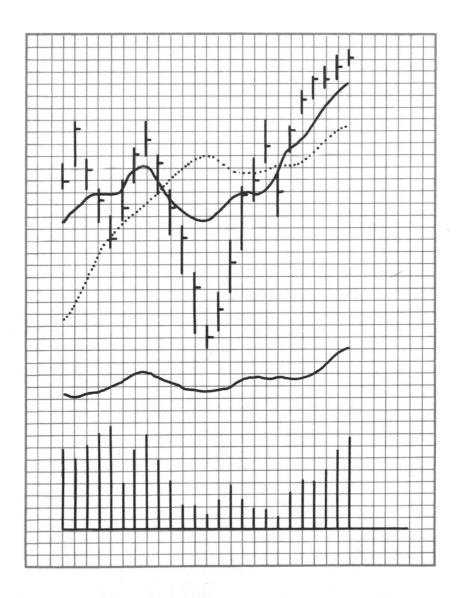

FIGURE 6-13   Answer to exercise.

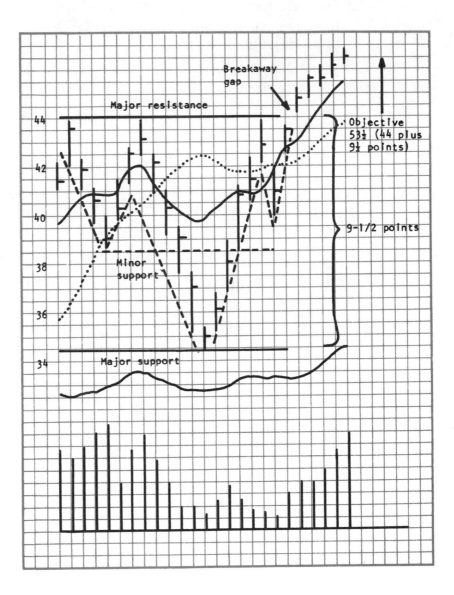

Falling Wedge

Price Action

Toward the end of a prolonged advance, the longs have big paper profits, and they are now looking to take some profits. Buyers get less aggressive, while sellers increase somewhat in numbers. For a period of three months or so, both the highs and the lows are lower. (See Figure 6-14.) The intermediate trend is down, but the prospect of a long-range upturn is not dead.

Volume

Preceding the wedge is sometimes a sharp increase in prices, which is accompanied by a burst of volume. During the wedge formation itself, however, volume is generally moderate with a small spike here or there. Light volume on minor selloffs is a bullish indicator. Look for heavy volume on the breakout.

Support/Resistance

Neither support nor resistance can be identified within the pattern itself. Support has to be found in preceding price activity. After a breakout, the formation itself may offer some resistance, but nothing very clear.

Moving Averages

The longer-term average flattens out, eventually converging with the 50-day MA and prices. The 50-day MA may even violate the longer average without significance. Watch for false breakouts.

Relative Strength

The trend is neutral. With the stock's price in a downtrend, this issue is in trouble.

FIGURE 6-14   Falling wedge.

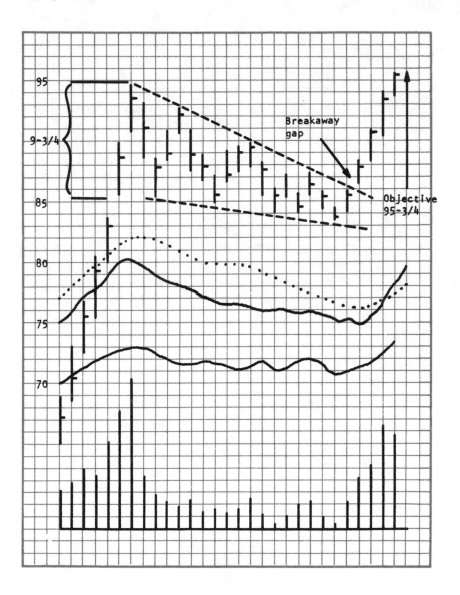

Forecasting Value

Look for a breakout on heavy volume about three-quarters of the way through the wedge. Add the greatest height of the wedge to the breakout point for an upside objective.

Upside Blowoff (Buying Panic)

Price Action

At or very close to the end of a major advance in prices may come the upside blowoff, which may be immediately preceded by falling flags or pennants. Peaking bullish sentiment is evident in the measuring (or runaway) gaps and ultimately an exhaustion gap that earmark an almost vertical trend—all in only a few days or up to several weeks. (See Figures 6-15 and 6-16.)

FIGURE 6-15
Price action preceding upside blowoff (buying panic).

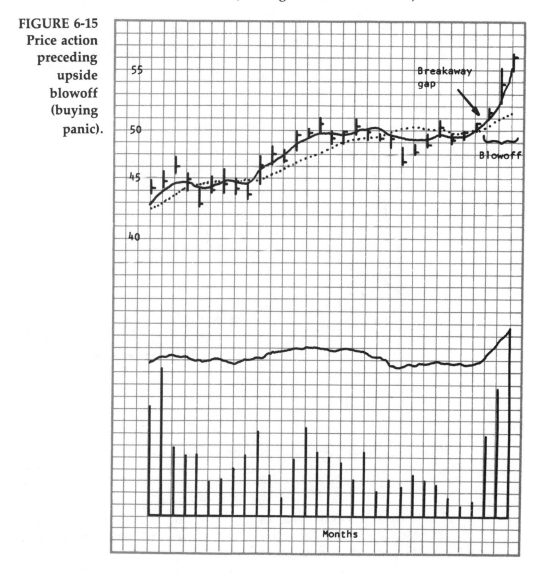

FIGURE 6-16   Upside blowoff (buying panic).

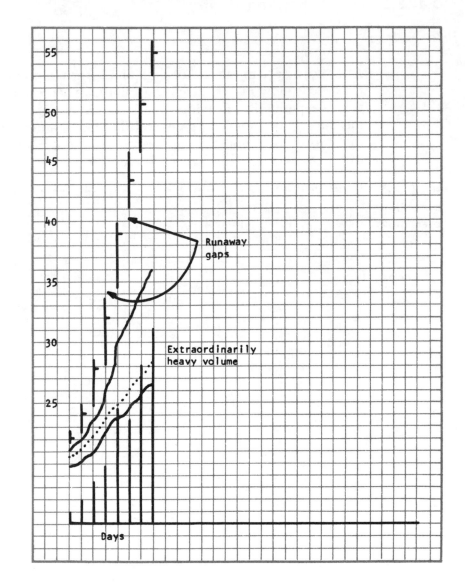

Volume

Explosive volume crests with the end of the formation.

Support/Resistance

The only support or resistance to be found is in past price action. The blowoff is so volatile that it can collapse without warning and without any discernible floor.

Moving Averages

When prices quickly move 35% to 50% over the 200-day moving average, look for the blowoff.

Relative Strength

This is of no help with prices moving so rapidly.

Forecasting Value

No firm objectives can be calculated. However, if prices rise sharply on heavy volume after a gap, a V top pattern might be in the making. (See Figure 6-17.)

FIGURE 6-17   V pattern in upside blowoff.

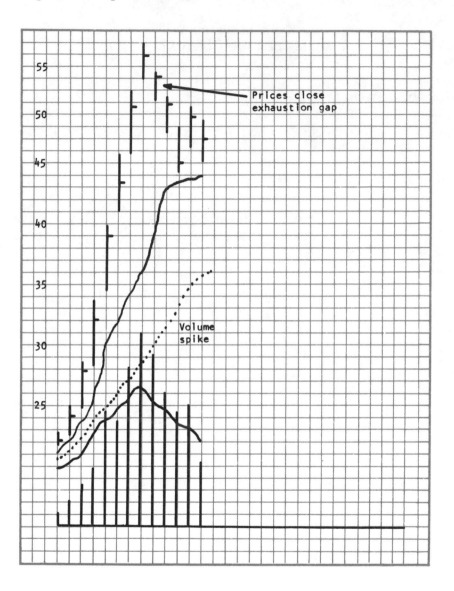

7

Distribution

When a stock has spent itself and the prolonged price advance draws to an end, the conditions are right for a major reversal. Before prices turn downward, however, the stock undergoes a distribution period. During this phase, the stock passes from holders who were once reluctant to sell because they anticipated ever higher prices to buyers who are less convinced that future prices will be much higher. The long-term result is that prices move horizontally in a lengthy neutral trend, eventually breaking downward. The generally accepted rule of thumb is that the longer the distribution phase, the longer the downtrend to follow.

In all the following patterns, once again common or ex-dividend gaps are meaningless. Breakaway gaps, however, are very helpful (when they occur) since they can be used as the breakout points in estimating price objectives.

V Top (Spike Top Reversal)

Price Action

Very aggressive buyers push prices up on the last day of a blowoff. On preceding days, prices have been soaring, and gaps have peppered the price action. On the day of the V top, the stock might open on a gap, or the opening might even be delayed. Quickly the exhaustion gap in the blowoff pattern is filled, as prices plummet, forming the second leg of an inverted V. (See Figure 7-1.) Things happen much too rapidly, however, for most nonprofessional chartists to react to such a pattern, much less profit by it. The only visible trend is short term—and it is down. There is not much that can be done during such a development, except to follow the price action and wait for less hair-rising times.

Sometimes prices come out of the dive to level off in a tight trading channel—a tail or handle (as in the V bottom pattern). The trend during this "extended V top," which could last up to two or three months, is intermediate neutral.

Volume

Volume spikes just as dramatically as prices—and too quickly to act as an indicator. If a handle develops, volume is moderate, with occasional bursts.

Support/Resistance

Prices and volume are too volatile, and events to rapid, to discern anything in the way of support or resistance.

In the event of a handle, major support can be found at the bottom of the pattern, but major resistance should not be expected below the topmost point of the V formation.

FIGURE 7-1   V top (spike top reversal).

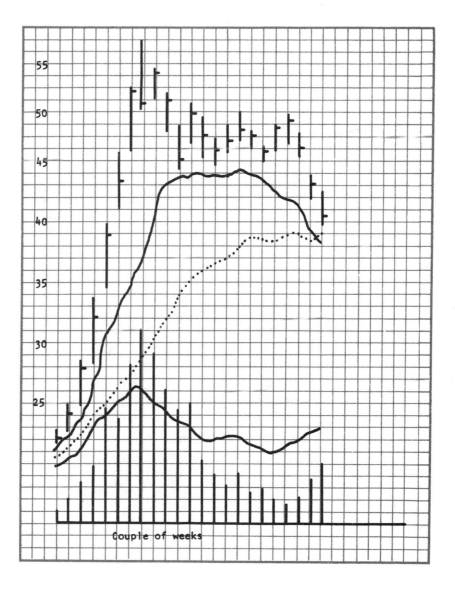

Moving Averages

The 50-day MA understandably remains above the longer average, but that is about all one can say.

In an extended V top, prices drop back toward the 200-MA, as you would expect. When the 50-day average crosses below the longer average, be alert for a bearish turn in prices.

Relative Strength

Instead of rolling over gently, RS forms a V top with prices. If the V top grows a handle (or tail), RS will eventually stabilize, telling nothing more about the future direction of prices.

Forecasting Value

There are no hard rules, just two general guidelines. One is that a severe downtrend, however short-term it may be, is imminent—within a day or days. The second is that, when prices move more than 25% over the 200-day MA, look for at least a technical correction.

Carefully chart the handle, if one develops. When a breakout downward occurs, measure the distance from the top of the V pattern to the support level in the handle. Then deduct that distance from the breakout point for a downside price objective.

Exercise

In Figure 7-1:

- Identify runaway gaps, the exhaustion gap, and the key reversal day.
- If possible, calculate a downside objective. If one is not possible, explain why.
- Compare your responses with Figure 7-2.

FIGURE 7-2   **7-2. Answer to exercise.**

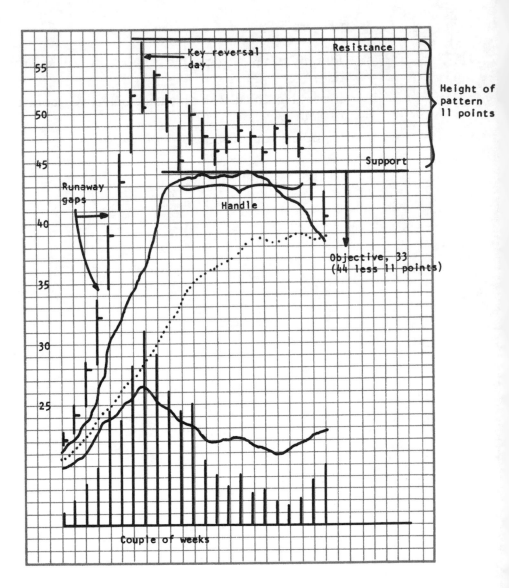

Double Top (M Pattern)

Price Action

Sometimes prices peak twice, forming a double inverted V, or M, pattern. (See Figure 7-3.) The big difference between the two formations is that, whereas the V pattern can happen in a day or so, the M takes at least two months—and often three or four months—to unfold. While the M develops, the trend is considered intermediate neutral, but the last leg can slide into a long-term downtrend.

Volume

Heaviest on the first V top, volume withers during the second part of the formation.

Support/Resistance

Major support is found along the "feet" of the pattern, while major resistance occurs along the top of it.

Moving Averages

During the first V, prices move well above the 200-day MA. If you can correctly identify the M pattern, there is a buying opportunity during the middle trough. After the second peak, the longer average flattens out. The 50-day MA may move over the 200-day average during the first V, but this is of no significance—a false signal. Watch for the bearish signal later in the formation when the shorter average crosses downward over the longer one.

Relative Strength

RS reaches its pinnacle before prices do.

FIGURE 7-3
Double top
(M pattern)

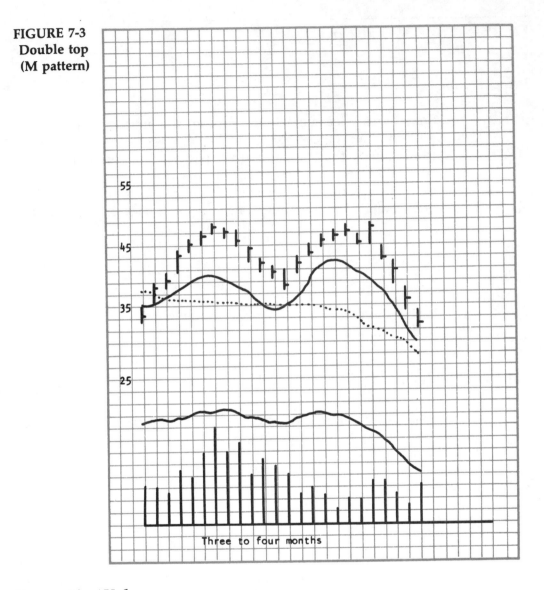

Three to four months

Forecasting Value

The middle trough is generally at least 10% to 15% lower than the two V's, so that it provides a buying opportunity for anyone who can recognize the pattern.

Once prices have broken through the support at the bottom of the M, calculate a downside objective by subtracting the height of the pattern (measured from the top of the V's to "feet") from the breakout point.

Triple Top

Price Action

If distribution is not complete by the time of the second peak in the M pattern, a third V may form: This so-called triple top may take up to six months to develop. (See Figure 7-4.) The third peak indicates that a long-term downtrend is in the making.

Volume

By the third peak, volume has all but dried up.

FIGURE 7-4   Triple top.

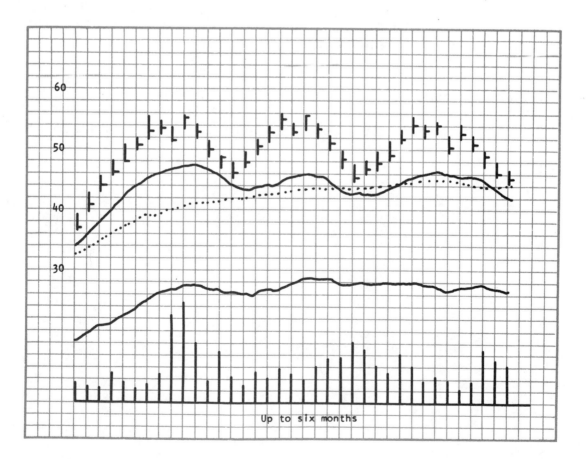

Support/Resistance

Support and resistance are the same as in an M pattern, but both are considered stronger for having been tested a third time. All the more reason to regard the ensuing downtrend as longlasting, having broken through such strong support.

Moving Averages

The averages may cross more than once, but these must be regarded as whipsaws.

Relative Strength

As prices move upward the third time, relative strength falters. If it surges while prices hesitate, perhaps the stock is one that will be the last to suffer in the coming bear market.

Forecasting Value

Once a breakout is evident, a downside objective is calculated just as in the M pattern.

Exercise

In Figure 7-4:

- Draw and label lines of support and resistance.
- Identify the breakout point.
- Calculate a downside objective.

    Compare your results with Figure 7-5.

FIGURE 7-5   Answer to exercise.

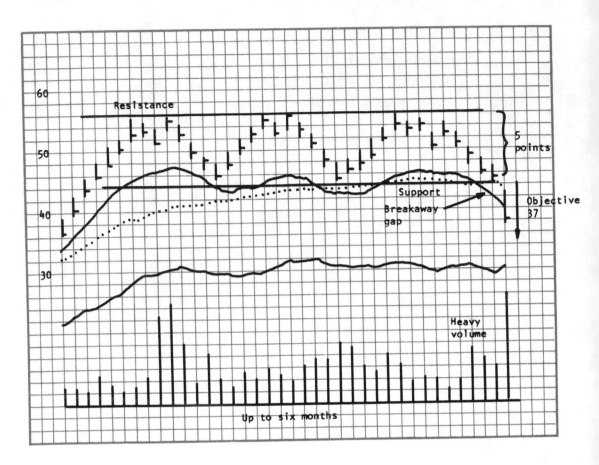

Head and Shoulders Top Pattern

Price Action

This very popular reversal pattern frequenty occurs after a prolonged advance. Over three to six months, the by now familiar
shoulder-head-shoulder develops with many minor up- and
downtrends. (See Figure 7-6.) The major trend, however, is neutral. The longs are liquidating their positions; prices are about to
move downward.

Volume

Typically in this formation, volume starts out heavy on the left
shoulder and diminishes throughout the pattern.

Support/Resistance

The neckline reflects major support. Minor resistance appears at
the tops of the shoulders, major resistance along the top of the
head.

Moving Averages

After some whipsaws, the 200-day MA flattens out. When the
short-term average crosses below the longer-term MA, look for the
breakout.

Relative Strength

At first flat, RS rises with the left shoulder and head, then turns
gradually downward with the right shoulder.

FIGURE 7-6   Head and shoulders top.

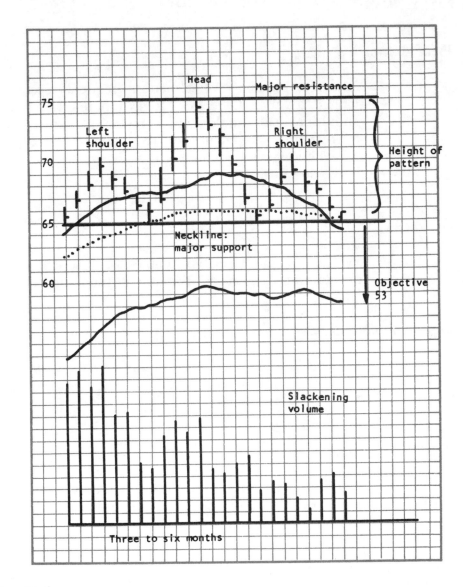

Forecasting Value

As in other types of head and shoulders patterns, deduct the height of the formation (from the head to the neckline) from the breakout point to arrive at a minimum price level.

Rectangular (Flat) Top Pattern

Price Action

In this easily identifiable configuration, highs and lows alternate within a horizontal channel, with a great deal more churning at the top than at the bottom. (See Figure 7-7.) This overall neutral formation, despite the numerous minor up- and downtrends, can take weeks or months to unfold. The longer it takes, the stronger the basis for the eventual downside movement.

FIGURE 7-7   **Rectangular (flat) top pattern.**

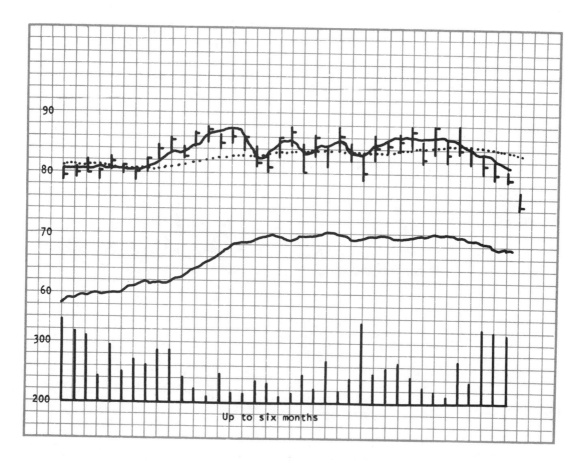

Volume

Activity expands when prices move lower, reflecting the increasing aggressiveness of sellers. It rises dramatically as the breakout occurs.

Support/Resistance

Support is very clear along the line connecting the lows. Just as evident is resistance along the highs.

Moving Averages

Throughout most of the pattern, there is the possibility of false signals. Prices moving below a declining 200-day MA, however, can usually be regarded as a sell signal. When the 50-day average crosses below the 200-day average, the sell signal is even stronger.

Relative Strength

RS moves laterally with prices.

Forecasting Value

Once the downward move is established, deduct the height of the pattern from the breakout point for the price objective.

Exercise

In Figure 7-7:

- Identify the lines of support and resistance.
- Is there a breakaway gap?
- Calculate a downside objective.

Compare your results with Figure 7-8.

FIGURE 7-8   Answer to exercise.

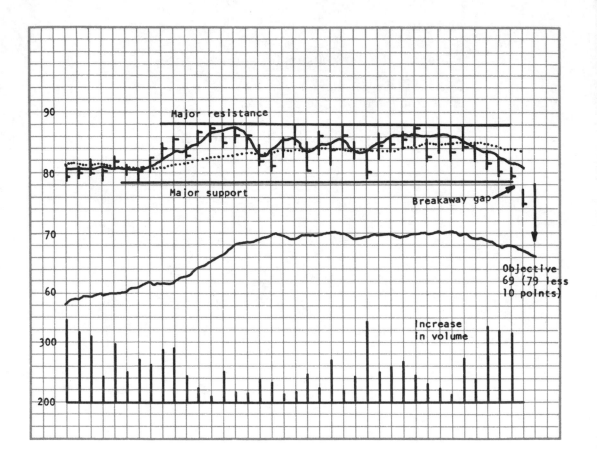

Broadening Top

Price Action

This confusing formation, the reverse of a symmetrical triangle, consists of higher highs and lower (and sometimes horizontal) lows. The textbook pattern consists of three highs and two lows. (See Figure 7-9.) Throughout the several months that this pattern takes to develop, the overall trend is difficult, if not impossible, to discern.

Volume

To confuse you even more, volume increases on both the highs and lows, eventually picking up with the breakout.

Support/Resistance

If the pattern assumes its typical "megahorn" shape, then there is no visible support. It becomes visible only if the the lows are horizontal. Resistance is generally not detectible at all.

Moving Averages

Amid many false moves, prices may touch the 200-day MA on the first low and penetrate it on the second low or on a breakout.

Relative Strength

The indication might be, with RS bending upward slightly throughout the price swings, that the stock is outperforming the market. But you have to be cautious during such an unsettled configuration.

Forecasting Value

There are no measurable objectives in this pattern.

FIGURE 7-9   Broadening top.

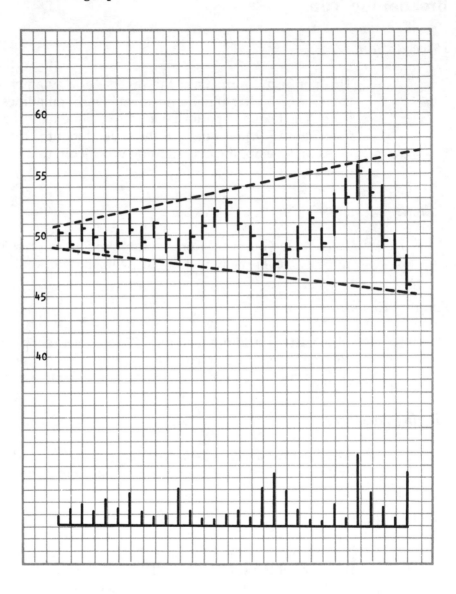

Diamond Top

Price Action

Over several months (and usually, but not always, at the tops of major markets), prices create higher highs and lower lows in a broadening pattern. Then the trading range gradually becomes constricted, after the highs hit a peak and the lows start trending upward. (The turning points for the highs and lows need not come at the same time.) Look for the diamond top formation in very active markets. (See Figure 7-10.)

FIGURE 7-10   Diamond top.

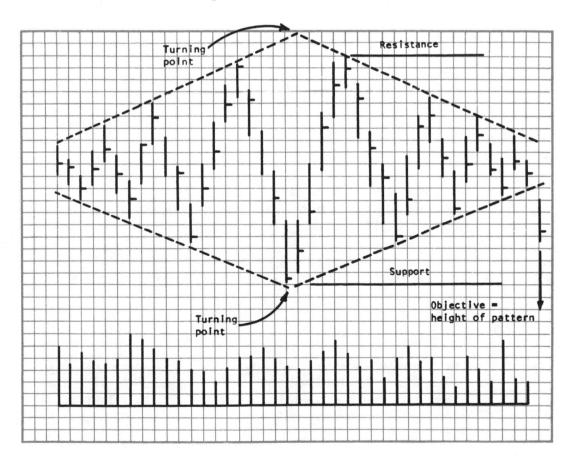

Volume

Activity stays high throughout.

Support/Resistance

Major support can be found at the turning point of the lows, major resistance at the top peak of the diamond.

Moving Averages

After some whipsawing, the 200-day average flattens out. Once that happens, watch for the 50-day MA to cross below it as a signal of the breakout.

Relative Strength

RS peaks before prices.

Forecasting Value

To forecast the minimum downside price level, add the height of the diamond (from turning point to turning point), and deduct it from the breakout point.

Saucer (Rounding Top) Pattern

Price Action

Prices slowly ascend, level off, and then turn downward lazily in this six-to seven-month pattern. Sometimes a handle forms as lows flatten out along a support level. (See Figure 7-11.) The trend is neutral.

FIGURE 7-11   Saucer (rounding top) pattern.

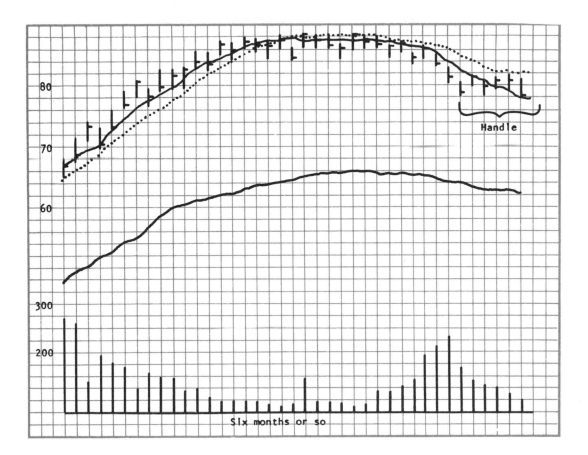

Volume

Volume mirrors price action—heavier at either end of the pattern than in the middle.

Support/Resistance

Support, if it is present at all, may be found along the base of the handle. Resistance is major along the top of the saucer, minor along the top of the handle.

Moving Averages

When the 50-day MA crosses below the long-term average, this is a sign of a downturn.

Relative Strength

RS tracks the rounding of prices.

Forecasting Value

Deduct the height of the pattern from the breakout point for a downside price level. Determining where the pattern begins is the hardest part of this calculation.

Exercise

In Figure 7-11:

- Draw vertical lines where you feel the saucer top begins and ends.
- Draw lines indicating where major support and resistance may be found, if anywhere.
- Calculate a downside price level.

  Compare your results with Figure 7-12.

FIGURE 7-12   Answer to exercise.

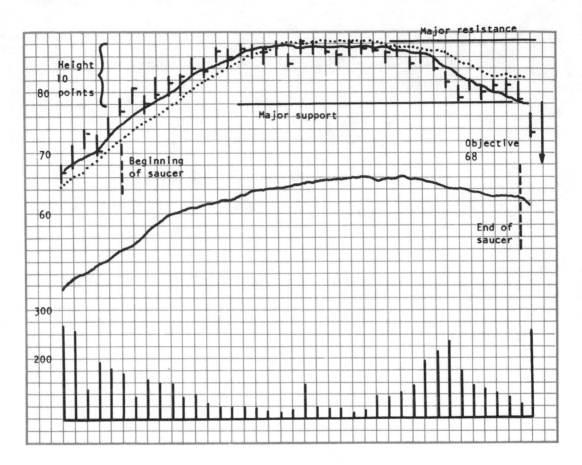

Island Reversal Top Pattern

Price Action

This blowoff, or buying panic, cannot be classified as a V top because it takes days—occasionally a couple of weeks—to develop. Prices quickly move up several points, leaving runaway and exhaustion gaps in their wake. As traders start to take profits, the trend is abruptly reversed, leaving an "island" of activity at the peak. After the accelerated minor uptrend, the long-term view is downward-sloped. (See Figure 7-13.)

**FIGURE 7-13
Island reversal
top pattern.**

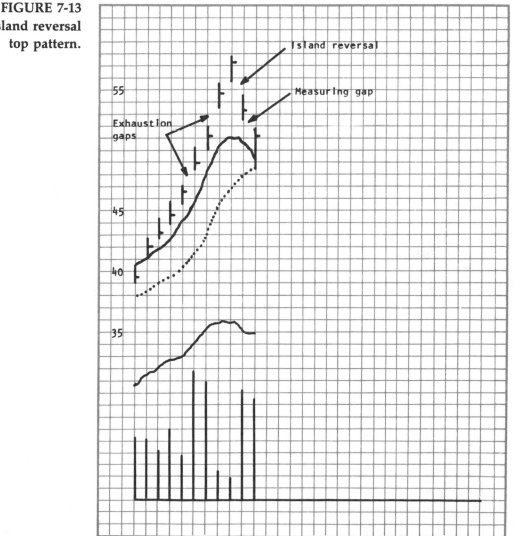

Volume

Although there is some expansion on the price rallies, volume picks up dramatically on the downside of the pattern.

Support/Resistance

Support is minor, if it exists at all. Resistance along the successive highs must also be considered minor. Only when prices turn downward can major resistance be identified at the peak of the formation.

Moving Averages

Expect a technical correction as prices move significantly above the long-term moving average.

Relative Strength

When RS fails to top out with prices, watch at least for a technical correction.

Forecasting Value

Beyond the inevitable correction due to the volatility of prices, no objectives can be calculated on the basis of this pattern.

8

The Markdown Phase

Marking the transition from distribution to markdown is the breaking of support. Once this event is identified, you can think in terms of a long-term decline in prices—lower highs, lower lows, occasional consolidations and minor rallies on light volume. Supply is becoming increasingly available, outweighing the possible demand in most cases.

As in the other three phases, common or ex-dividend gaps are generally meaningless. The breakaway gap at the commencement of this phase, however, signals the beginning of the markdown.

Rising Flag

Price Action

Early in the markdown phase, a sharp drop in prices reflects the activity of traders who are taking advantage of the selloff, driving prices down, and creating a "pole." (See Figure 8-1.) Since the pole forms as the result of short-term trading, a minor rally is all but inevitable, and it takes the form of a brief upward-sloping channel. While the pole can form in days, the whole formation takes no more than a couple of weeks. Near term, the outlook is neutral, but the long-term trend is still the same—down.

FIGURE 8-1   Rising flag.

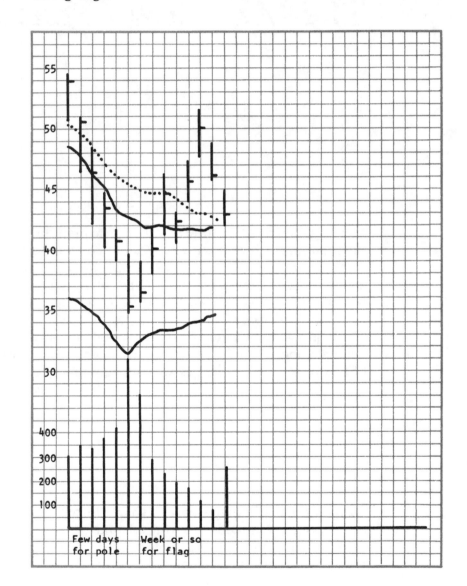

Volume

As the pole forms, volume is heavy, but it slacks off during the rally, a weak response to the selloff. With the breakout downward, volume picks up again.

Support/Resistance

Look for major support prior to the rising flag pattern and for minor support at the bottom of the pole. Major resistance is obvious at the peak of the configuration.

Moving Averages

While the pole easily penetrates the 200-day MA, the flag may rise enough to touch it. When prices and the average come together, you may have a selling opportunity.

Relative Strength

RS declines sharply with prices. If it does not respond in an upward direction, it may be indicating a downturn.

Forecasting Value

Look for a short-term 50% retracement of the pole. Longer term, deduct the height of the pole from the breakout point for a downside price objective.

Exercise

In Figure 8-1:

- Identify the pole and draw the trend- and channel lines outlining the flag.
- Draw lines of support and resistance, if any.
- Calculate the long-term price objective.

Compare your responses to Figure 8-2.

FIGURE 8-2　Answer to exercise.

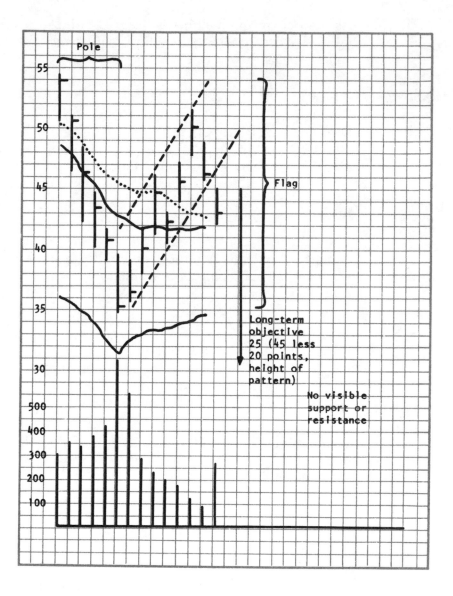

Pennant

Price Action

A pennant sometimes follows a flag. As prices break downward out of the flag's channel, they form a second pole. The action mimics that of the flag, with the exception that the rally activity truncates in a series of lower highs and higher lows—all in only a few days. (See Figure 8-3.) During this price consolidation, the minor trend is neutral.

Volume

The activity is the same as it is for the flag.

Support/Resistance

Do not look for support within the pennant. Minor support might be found within the flag, major support sometime prior to the flag. Major resistance is likely to be found at the support level of the flag.

Moving Averages

The pole may again penetrate the 200-day MA, but the pennant will probably not touch it.

Relative Strength

Momentum has developed for an accelerating downtrend.

FIGURE 8-3   Pennant.

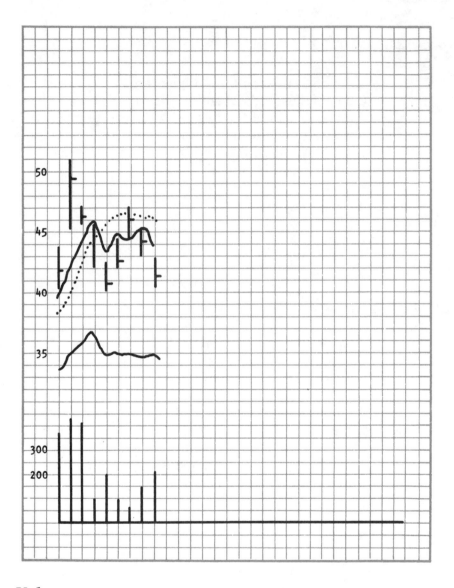

Forecasting Value

Look for a breakaway gap to signal the onset of a major decline. Once that occurs, you can estimate short-term objectives. Given three runaway gaps (include the breakaway as one), measure the distance between the first two gaps and deduct it from the third. The result is the short-term price objective.

Exercise

In Figure 8-3:

- Identify support and resistance (major or minor), if any.
- Draw the lines tracing out the pennant.

    Compare your results with Figure 8-4.

FIGURE 8-4   Answer to exercise.

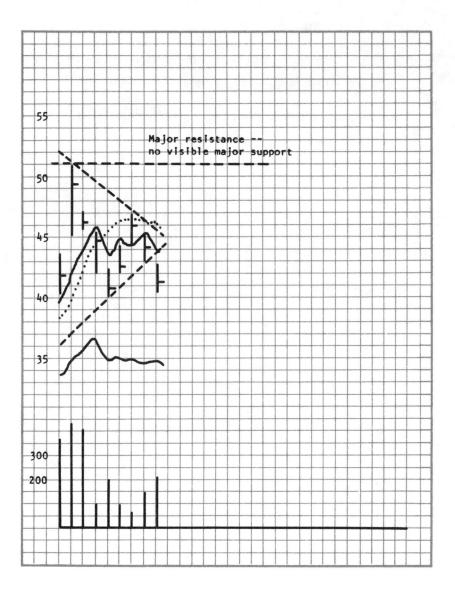

Symmetrical Coil

Price Action

Although it is not preceded by a pole, the coil develops very much like the rally in the pennant—in a series of lower highs and higher lows. Taking several weeks to several months to unfold amid a number of whipsaws, this consolidating formation reflects a minor and intermediate neutral trend. While the long-term outlook is down, this pattern contains nothing that would indicate a long-range trend in any direction, it is that neutral. (See Figure 8-5.)

Volume

Moderate throughout the pattern, with random spurts of activity, volume expands with the breakout.

Support/Resistance

Minor support levels are created at the successively higher lows, but major support is found only at the base of the coil. At the top of the coil, resistance is major.

Moving Averages

The 200-day average slowly converges with prices. A crossover with prices about three-quarters of the way through the formation may be considered a sell signal.

Relative Strength

The flattening out of this line can indicate that the stock and the market are performing on the same footing.

FIGURE 8-5   Symmetrical coil.

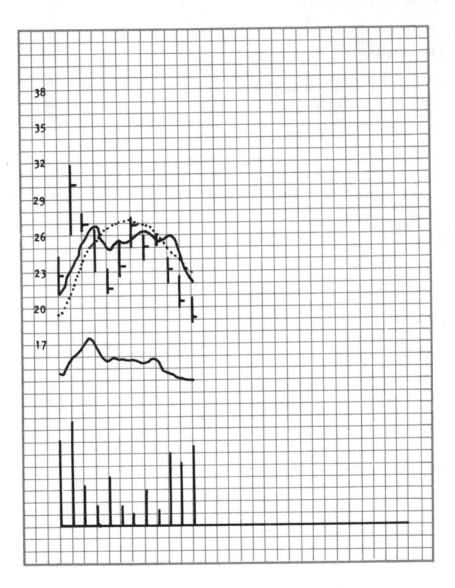

Forecasting Value

Watch for a breakout about three-quarters of the way through the coil, sometimes on a breakaway gap. Add the height of the coil at the open end to the breakout point for a downside price objective.

Exercise

In Figure 8-5:

• Draw the trend- and channel lines outlining the coil.
• Identify levels of support and resistance (major or minor), if any.
• Calculate the price objective.

Compare your results with Figure 8-6.

FIGURE 8-6   Answer to exercise.

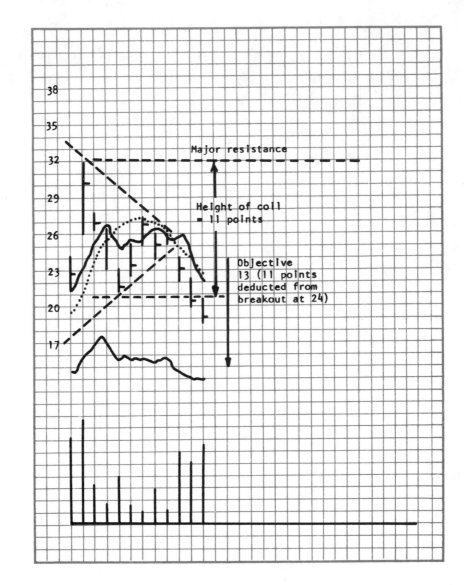

Rising Wedge

Price Action

Very close to the end of the markdown phase, prices may go through a period in which both successive highs and successive lows are higher, with the overall pattern drifting upward. (See Figure 8-7.) For a while, sellers are less aggressive, giving whatever weak demand that is out there an opportunity to move prices slightly upward in the short run. Over the weeks or months that this pattern takes to unwind, the near and intermediate trend is clearly upward, but the long-range outlook is still down.

Volume

Activity diminishes as the pattern develops, indicating its contrarian nature.

Support/Resistance

Besides a series of minor support levels at the lows, there is not major support to be found. Neither is any resistance detectable in the configuration.

Moving Averages

The upward penetration of the 200-day MA by prices has to be regarded as a false bull signal.

Relative Strength

RS rounds with prices.

FIGURE 8-7   Rising wedge.

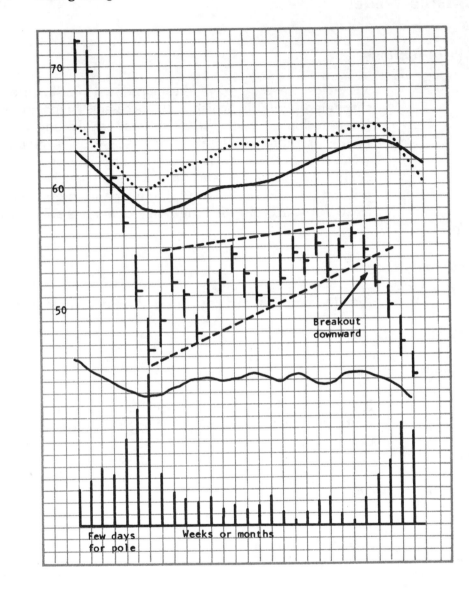

Forecasting Value

As in the pennant or coil, watch for a breakout about three-quarters of the way through the formation. Deduct the open-end height of the wedge from the breakout out for the objective.

Descending Triangle

Price Action

Over a period that runs, on average, four to six weeks, prices go into a steep dive, forming a pole. They then taper off into a tight trading range, characterized by lower highs and a line of horizontal lows. While the pole represents a marked downtrend, the triangle, retracing a third to a half of the pole, is considered neutral. (See Figure 8-8.)

Volume

Although heavy as the pole forms, volume dries up during the triangle.

Support/Resistance

Major support is discernible along the lows. While some minor resistance might be identified along the descending highs, no major resistance is to be found.

Moving Averages

The two averages track prices, eventually converging and prices pull back.

Relative Strength

Like the averages, RS follows the path of prices, eventually going flat as the triangle forms.

FIGURE 8-8   Descending triangle.

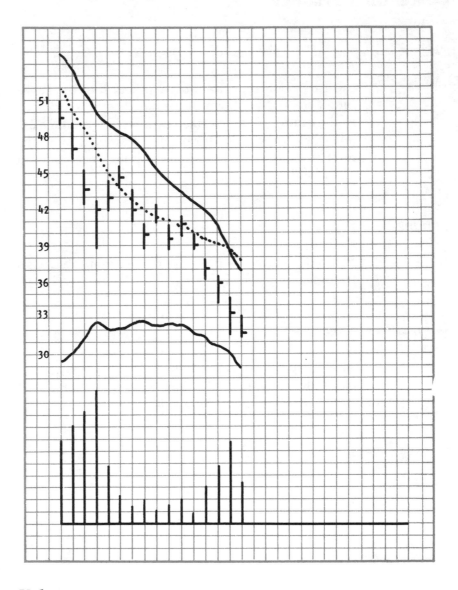

Forecasting Value

Again, watch for downside penetration three-quarters of the way through the pattern. To arrive at an objective, deduct the open-end height of the triangle to the downside breakout point.

Exercise

In Figure 8-8:

- Identify the pole, and draw the lines outlining the descending triangle.
- Locate the breakaway gap.
- Estimate a price objective.

    Compare your responses with Figure 8-9.

FIGURE 8-9   Answer to exercise.

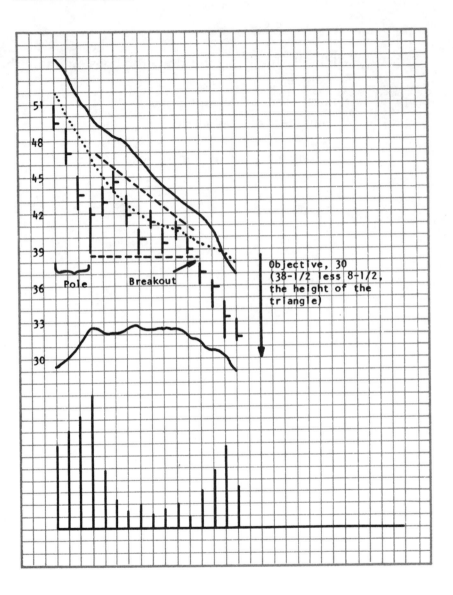

Continuation Head and Shoulders

Price Action

Although not truly a markdown pattern, this formation—normally part of a reversal—occasionally shows up in a continuation or consolidation role. (See Figure 8-10.) Although sometimes in this version prices may rally back to the neckline after the completion of the right shoulder, this is not to be taken as a bullish signal. Within the configuration, the minor trends may be up or down, and the intermediate trend is neutral. Ultimately, however, prices are destined to resume their major descent.

FIGURE 8-10   Continuation head and shoulders.

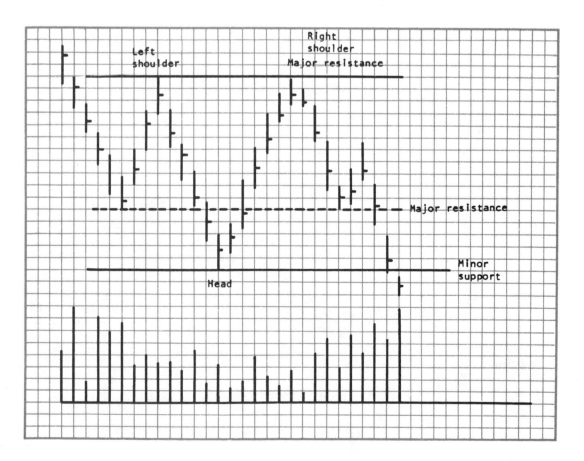

Volume

> Atypically for a head and shoulders, volume undergoes random peaks and troughs.

Support/Resistance

> Support is evident along the horizontal lows. Resistance is minor at the peaks of the shoulders, major at the top of the head.

Moving Averages/Relative Strength

> Flattened out, neither the averages nor relative strength is of any help.

Forecasting Value

> When prices penetrate the neckline, deduct the height of the pattern (from the head to the neckline) from the breakout level for the price objective.

Blowoff (Selling Climax)

Price Action

> Toward the very end of the markdown phase, aggressive sellers flood the market, sending prices "over the falls." For the several days to few weeks taken up by this volatile pattern—which is awash with runaway gaps—there is only one trend, and that is down. (See Figure 8-11.)

Volume

> Record levels may be attained.

FIGURE 8-11   Blowoff (selling climax).

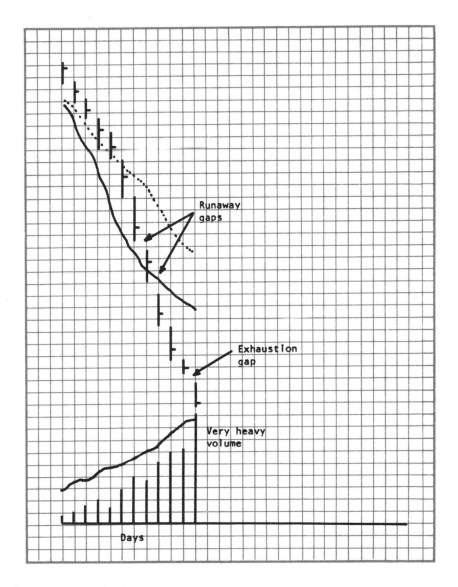

Support/Resistance

Neither support nor resistance is visible within the formation. The only real support might not be found for months or a year prior to this cascade of prices. Resistance is nowhere in sight.

Moving Averages

At best, you might take advantage of an oversold situation. If prices are more than 50% out of line with the 200-day MA, look for an oversold rally.

Relative Strength

RS dips with prices, but it is of little help.

Forecasting Value

Lasting price objectives are difficult, if not impossible, to estimate. About the best you can do is estimate fleeting, short-term objectives by watching the gaps. Specifically, given three runaway gaps (counting the breakaway as one), deduct the distance between the first two gaps from the third one for a quick objective.

Sources of Information

Allen, R. C. *How to Use the 4 Day, 9 Day and 18 Day Moving Averages to Earn Larger Profits from Commodities*. Chicago: Best Books, 1974.

Arms, Richard W. *Volume Cycles in the Stock Market: Market Timing Through Equivolume Charting*. Homewood, IL: Dow Jones-Irwin, 1983.

Belveal, L. Dee. *Charting Commodity Market Price Behavior*, 2nd edition. Homewood, IL: Dow Jones-Irwin, 1985.

Bernstein, Jacob. *The Handbook of Commodity Cycles: a Window on Time*. New York: Wiley, 1982.

Bolton, A. Hamilton. *The Elliott Wave Principle: a Critical Appraisal*. Hamilton, Bermuda: Monetary Research, 1960.

Blumenthal, Earl. *Chart for Profit Point & Figure Trading*. Larchmont, NY: Investors Intelligence, 1975.

Bressert, Walter J. and James Hardie Jones. *The HAL Blue Book: How to Use Cycles with an Overbought/Oversold and Momentum Index for More Consistent Profits*. Tucson, AZ: HAL Market Cycles, 1984.

Cohen, A. W. *How to Use the Three-Point Reversal Method of Point & Figure Stock Market Trading*, 8th revised edition. Larchmont, NY: Chartcraft, 1982.

Cootner, Paul H. (ed.). *The Random Character of Stock Market Prices*. Cambridge, MA: MIT Press, 1964.

de Villiers, Victor. *The Point and Figure Method of Anticipating Stock Price Movements: Complete Theory and Practice.* Brightwaters, NY: Windsor Books, orig. 1933; reprinted in 1975.

Dewey, Edward R. with Og Mandino. *Cycles, the Mysterious Forces That Trigger Events.* New York: Manor Books, 1973.

Dunn & Hargitt. *Point and Figure Commodity Trading: a Computer Evaluation.* Lafayette, IN: Dunn & Hargitt, 1971.

Dunn & Hargitt, *Trader's Notebook: Trading Methods Checked by Computer.* Lafayette, IN: Dunn & Hargitt, 1970.

Edwards, Robert D. and John Magee, *Technical Analysis of Stock Trends,* 5th ed. Boston: John Magee, 1966.

Elliott, Ralph N. (edited by Robert Prechter). *The Major Works of R. N. Elliott.* Chappaqua, NY: New Classics Library, 1980.

Emery, Walter L. (ed.). *Commodity Year Book.* Jersey City, NJ: Commodity Research Bureau, published annually.

Frost, Alfred J. and Robert R. Prechter. *Elliott Wave Principle, Key to Stock Market Profits.* Chappaqua, NY: New Classics Library, 1978.

Gann, W. D. *How to Make Profits in Commodities,* rev. ed. Pomeroy, WA: Lambert-Gann Publishing, orig. 1942; reprinted in 1976.

Hadady, R. Earl. *Contrary Opinion: How to Use It for Profit in Trading Commodity Futures.* Pasadena, CA: Hadady Publications, 1983.

Hurst, J. M. *The Profit Magic of Stock Transaction Timing.* Englewood Cliffs, NJ: Prentice-Hall, 1970.

Jiler, Harry (ed.). *Guide to Commodity Price Forecasting.* New York: Commodity Research Bureau, 1971.

Jiler, William L. *How Charts Can Help You in the Stock Market.* New York: Trendline, 1962.

Kaufman, Perry J. *Commodity Trading Systems and Methods.* New York: Wiley, 1978.

Kaufmann, Perry J. *Technical Analysis in Commodities.* New York: Wiley, 1980.

Murphy, John J. *Technical Analysis of the Futures Markets.* New York: New York Institute of Finance, 1986.

Patel, Charles. *Technical Trading Systems for Commodities and Stocks.* Walnut Creek, CA: Trading Systems Research, 1980.

Pring, Martin. *Technical Analysis Explained,* 2nd ed. New York: McGraw-Hill, 1985.

Schultz, John W. *The Intelligent Chartist.* New York: WRSM Financial Services, 1962.

Schwager, Jack D. *A Complete Guide to the Futures Markets: Fundamental Analysis, Technical Analysis, Trading, Spreads, and Options.* New York: Wiley, 1984.

Sklarew, Arthur. *Techniques of a Professional Commodity Chart Analyst.* New York: Commodity Research Bureau, 1980.

Teweles, Richard J., Charles V. Harlow, and Herbert L. Stone. *The Commodity Futures Game–Who Wins?–Who Loses?–Why?* 2nd ed. New York: McGraw-Hill, 1974.

Vodopich, Donald R. *Trading for Profit with Precision Timing.* Atlanta: Precision Timing, 1984.

Wheelan, Alexander H. *Study Helps in Point and Figure Technique.* Morgan Rogers, 1966.

Wilder, J. Welles. *New Concepts in Technical Trading Systems.* Greensboro, NC: Trend Research, 1978.

Williams, Larry R. *How I Made $1,000,000 Trading Commodities Last Year,* 3rd ed. Monterey, CA: Conceptual Management, 1979.

Zieg, Kermit C., Jr., and Perry J. Kaufman. *Point and Figure Commodity Trading Techniques.* Larchmont, NY: Investors Intelligence, 1975.

Glossary

Accelerating trend A trend whose slope, whether up or down, is increasing sharply. (Most valid trendlines rise at an angle approximating 45 degrees.) In an accelerating trend, sometimes several trendlines may have to be drawn at increasingly steeper angles. Some chartists advocate the use of a curving trendline in such cases.

Accumulation phase The first phase of a major trend, which represents informed buying by the most astute investors as all the so-called "bad economic news" has finally been discounted by the market.

See also Major trend.

Alteration rule (or principle) Holds that the market usually doesn't act the same way two times in a row. If a certain type of top or bottom occurred the last time around, it will probably not do so again this time. The rule of alteration doesn't tell us exactly what will happen, but tells us what probably won't.

Apex In a triangle, the point of intersection where the two lines meet. In a wedge formation, the apex is identified by two converging trendlines.

Arithmetic mean The average of a series of quantities, calculated by summing all the quantities and then dividing the total by the number of the qualities included in the average.

Also known as simple moving average.

Ascending triangle A pattern in which the upper trendline is flat, while the lower line is rising. This pattern indicates that buyers are more aggressive than sellers. It is considered a bullish pattern and is usually resolved with a breakout to the upside.

Bar chart A chart in which the vertical axis (the y axis) shows a scale representing the price of the contract, the horizontal axis (the x axis) records the passage of time, and dates are marked along the bottom of chart. All the user has to do is plot a vertical bar in the appropriate day from the day's high to the day's low (called the range). Then, place a small horizontal tic to the right of the vertical bar identifying the daily closing price. A bar chart is both a price and time chart.

Base In a triangle, a vertical line, measuring the height of the pattern, is called the *base*.

Black box approach An approach to technical analysis in primarily mechanical systems are used in analyzing trends.

Blowoffs Event at a major market top, in which prices suddenly begin to rally sharply after a long advance, accompanied by a large jump in trading activity. In futures trading, it is also accompanied by a sizable decline in the open interest.

Bottom failure swing An event in which the relative strength index (RSI) is in a downtrend (under 30), fails to set a new low, and then proceeds to exceed a previous peak.

Bottom reversal day At the end of a downtrend, the day on which a new low during the day is followed by a higher close.

Bottom reversal pattern A pattern in which prices hold above the previous low. The bottom is confirmed when the previous peak is overcome.

Bowl reversal pattern *See* Saucer reversal pattern.

Box size The value, expressed in terms of units of trading, assigned to each box on a point and figure chart. The smaller the value, the more sensitive the box is to price movement.

Breakaway gap A gap that occurs at the completion of an important price pattern and usually signals the beginning of a significant market move. Breakaway gaps usually occur on heavy volume.

Breakdown, point This is seen in a double top where there is a peak, trough, peak and the breakdown occurs after it descends below the first trough.

Broadening formation An inverted triangle or a triangle turned backwards, in which the trendlines actually diverge in the broadening formation, creating a picture that looks like an expanding triangle. Volume tends to expand along with the wider price swings.

Buffer zone   By using filters, you create a buffer or neutral zone between the upper envelope line and the moving average. No action is taken between the two lines. A buy signal is generated above the upper line, and the position is liquidated or stopped out on a close below the moving average.

Bull trap   An event in which prices break out in an upward direction and then down again, "trapping" some bulls.

Catapult   A breakout (or catapult) over the top of a congestion area.

Centering of average   The statistically correct way to plot a moving average is to *center* it. That means to place it in the middle of the time period it covers. *Centering* the average, however, has the major flaw of producing much later trend change signals.

Channel line   A line paralleling the trendline. It is drawn by drawing a parallel line through the point farthest away from the trendline. In an uptrend, the channel line is drawn through the lowest trough; in a down trend, through the highest peak. The *channel line*, or the *return line* as it is sometimes called, has measuring implications. Once a breakout occurs from an existing price channel, prices usually travel a distance equal to the width of the channel (that is, the distance between the trendline and channel line).

Chartist   Another term for technical analyst, because charts, whether handmade or computer-generated, are the primary working tool used for analysis.

Commodity Research Bureau (CRB) Price Index   The most widely followed barometer of commodity prices, this index measures the trend performance of 27 commodity futures markets.

Common gap   A gap that usually occurs in very thinly traded markets or in the middle of horizontal trading ranges. It is more a symptom of lack of interest than anything else.

Complex head and shoulders   An uncommon in which pattern two heads may appear or a double left and right shoulder. It has the same forecasting implications as a regular head and shoulder pattern.

Confirmation   The comparison of all technical signals and indicators to ensure that most of those indicators are pointing in the same direction and are confirming one another.

Congestion area   A period of horizontal or sideways price movement on the chart within a well-defined top and bottom. The main purpose of congestion area analysis is to help the analyst determine in advance the direction of the ultimate breakout.

Continuation pattern   Any pattern that typically signals the continuation of the trend in progress.

Contrary opinion, principle of   Holds that, when the vast majority of people agree on anything, they are generally wrong. A true contrarian will therefore first try to determine what the majority are doing and then will act in the opposite direction.

Correction   *See* Retracement.

Daily bar chart   A bar chart in which each vertical bar represents a day's price action: high, low, and closing prices. The tic to the right of the vertical bar is the closing price.

Danger zones   Price movement zones in which extremely overbought or oversold conditions prevail.

Descending triangle   This is a mirror image of the ascending triangle, and is generally considered a bearish pattern. This pattern indicates that sellers are more aggressive than buyers, and is usually resolved on the downside. The downside signal is registered by a decisive close under the lower trendline, usually on increased volume.

Detrending cycles   Moving averages have the effect of smoothing or eliminating shorter-term cycles, while allowing longer-range cycles to come through. Detrending reverses that process by eliminating cycles longer than the length of the average while shorter-term cycles become more visible. This is accomplished in effect by eliminating the influence of trend.

Diamond formation   This pattern is peculiar in that it is actually a combination of two different types of triangles—the *expanding* and the *symmetrical*. The diverging trendlines followed by converging trendlines from a chart picture resembling diamond. The volume pattern conforms to the price action by expanding during the first half of the pattern and then gradually declining as the price swings narrow in the second half of the formation.

Divergence   A situation where different delivery months or related markets or technical indicators fail to confirm one another.

Double crossover method A buy signal is produced when the shorter average crosses above the longer. This technique of using two averages together lags the market a bit more than the use of a single average but produces fewer whipsaws.

Double top or bottom Next to the *head and shoulders*, the most frequently seen and the most easily recognized. For obvious reasons, the top is often referred to as an "M" and the bottom as a "W." The general characteristics of a *double top* are similar to that of the head and shoulders and triple top except that only two peaks appear instead of three. The volume pattern is similar as is the measuring rule.

Downtrend A series of descending peaks and troughs.

Dow Theory

1. *The Averages Discount Everything*—every possible factor affecting supply and demand must be reflected in the market averages.

2. *The Market Has Three Trends*—*the primary, secondary, and minor.* An uptrend has a pattern of rising peaks and troughs. A downtrend would be just the opposite with successively lower peaks and troughs.

3. *Major Trends Have Three Phases*—the accumulation phase, represents informed buying. The second phase, where most technical trend-followers begin to participate, takes place as prices begin to advance rapidly. The final phase is characterized by informed investors who begin to "distribute" when no one else does.

4. *The Averages Must Confirm Each Other*—no important bull or bear market signal could take place unless both averages gave the same signal.

5. *Volume Must Confirm the Trend*—*volume should expand in the direction of the major trend.* It is an important factor in confirming the signals generated on the price charts.

6. *A Trend Is Assumed to Be in Effect Until It Gives Definite Signals That It Has Reversed.*

Efficient market hypothesis Prices fluctuate randomly about their intrinsic value. This theory also holds that the best market strategy to follow would be a simple "buy and hold" strategy as opposed to any attempt to "beat the market."

Exhaustion gap Appears near the end of a market move. After all objectives have been achieved and the other two types of gaps (breakaway and runaway) have been identified, the analyst should begin to expect the *exhaustion gap.*

Exponentially smoothed moving average The exponentially smoothed average assigns a greater weight to the more recent action. Therefore, it is a *weighted* moving average. But while it assigns diminished importance to past price action, it does include in its calculation all of the price data in the life of the futures contract.

Extended V reversal pattern Basically the same as the V pattern except that a small platform forms shortly after the market turns. The platform usually forms on the right-hand side of the chart.

Failed head and shoulder This pattern starts out looking like a classic head and shoulders reversal, but at some point in its development (either prior to the breaking of the neckline or just after it), prices resume their original trend.

Flag Preceded by a sharp and almost straight line move, a situation in which a steep advance or decline has gotten ahead of itself and where the market pauses briefly to "catch its breath" before running off again in the same direction. The flag resembles a parallelogram of rectangle marked by two parallel trendlines that tend to slope against the prevailing trend. In a downtrend, the flag would have a slight upward slope.

Fulcrum A well-defined congestion area, occurring after a significant advance or decline, that forms an accumulation base or a distribution top.

Fundamental analysis A type of analysis that focuses on the economic forces of supply and demand that cause prices to move higher, lower, or stay the same. The fundamental approach examines all of the relevant factors affecting the price of a commodity in order to determine the intrinsic value of that commodity.

Gaps These are simply areas on the bar chart where no trading has taken place.

Head and shoulders reversal pattern A series of peaks and troughs that resembles a three-pointed crown with the peaks on either side somewhat lower, forming the shoulders. The middle peak is called the head. The sequence is shoulder, head, shoulder. If the trend lines goes below the last shoulder trough then a downward trend may occur. This should be a warning to the investor that something is wrong.

High-low band When using filters for moving averages this is constructed by applying the same moving average to the high and low prices instead of to the closing price. The result is two moving average lines—one of the highs and one of the lows.

Horizontal axis (x axis)   Records the passage of time. Dates are marked along the bottom of the daily bar chart.

Intra-day bar chart   A type of bar chart that presents price action for a period of less than one day.

Inverse head and shoulders   A pattern with three distinct bottoms and a head (middle trough) a bit lower than either of the two shoulders. A decisive close through the neckline is also necessary to complete the pattern. Volume plays a much more critical role in the identification and completion of a head and shoulders bottom.

Island reversal   Sometimes after the upward exhaustion gap has formed, prices will trade in a narrow range for a couple of days or a week before gapping to the downside. Such a situation leaves the few days of price action looking like an "island" surrounded by space or water.

Key reversal day   The true *key reversal day* marks an important turning point, but cannot be correctly identified as such until well after the fact—that is, after prices have moved significantly in the opposite direction of the prior trend.

Line chart   This type of chart produces a solid line by connecting only the closing prices. Only the closing price is plotted for each successive day. Many chartists believe that because the closing price is the most critical price of the trading day, a line (or close-only) chart is a more valid measure of price activity.

Long-term charts   Weekly and monthly charts that compress price action in such a way that the time horizon can be greatly expanded and much longer time periods can be studied. Long-range price charts provide a perspective on the market trend that is impossible to achieve with the use of daily charts alone.

Major trend   Also known as a primary trend. It usually lasts longer than one year.

Measuring gap   *See* Runaway gap.

Minor trend   The *minor*, or *near-term*, *trend* usually lasts less than three weeks and represents shorter term fluctuations in the intermediate trend.

Moving average   An *average* of a certain body of data. The most common way to calculate the moving average is to work from the total of the last ten days' closing prices. Each day the new close is added to the total and the close 11 days back is subtracted. The new total is then divided by the umber of days (ten). The moving average is essentially a trend-following device. The most commonly used averages are five, ten, 20, and 40 days or some variation of those numbers (such as four, nine, and 18).

Near-term trend Also known as a minor trend. It usually lasts two or three weeks.

Neckline A line with a slight upward slope at the top often used in head and shoulders patterns. It helps to determine the completion of a pattern. When the trendline breaks the neckline a downward trend in the market could be developing.

Objective The price level projected on the basis of the current pattern.

O column On a point and figure chart, represents declining prices.

Open interest The total number of outstanding or unliquidated contracts at the end of the day. Open interest represents the total number of outstanding longs or shorts in the market, *not the sum of both*. Open interest has very definite seasonal tendencies that should be taken into consideration.

1. *Rising open interest in an uptrend is bullish.*
2. *Declining open interest in an uptrend is bearish.*
3. *Rising open interest in a downtrend is bearish.*
4. *Declining open interest in a downtrend is bullish.*

Oscillators The oscillator is extremely useful in nontrending markets where prices fluctuate in a horizontal price band, or trading range, creating a market situation where most trend-following systems simply don't work that well. Most oscillators look very much alike. They are plotted along the bottom of the daily price chart and resemble a flat horizontal bond. The oscillator band is basically flat while prices may be trading up, down, or sideways. However, the peaks and troughs in the oscillator coincide with the peaks and troughs on the price chart. Some oscillators have a midpoint value that divides the horizontal range into two halves, an upper and a lower. This midpoint line is usually a zero line.

Outright trading *Outright trading* refers to the taking of long or short positions in anticipation of a price rise or decline. The trader stands to benefit from an absolute change in price.

Outside day   A day when the high and low on the reversal day exceed the range of the previous day.

Pennant   A horizontal pattern identified by two converging trendlines. It is preceded by a sharp and almost straight line move. It represents a situation where a steep advance or decline has gotten ahead of itself and where the market pauses briefly to "catch its breath" before running off again in the same direction.

Percentage retracement   Prices retrace a portion of the previous trend before resuming the move in the original direction. These countertrend moves tend to fall into certain predictable percentage parameters. The best known application of the phenomenon is the *50% retracement.*

Platform   Sometimes just after the midpoint of the saucer bottom, a sudden spurt in prices on uncharacteristically heavy volume occurs after which prices return to the slow rounding process. A *handle* or *platform* sometimes appears toward the end of the base, followed by resumption of the new uptrend.

Point and figure chart   A type of chart that shows price action in a compressed format. It is made up of alternating column of x's and o's. The x columns show rising prices and the o columns, declining prices. Buy and sell signals are more precise and easier to spot on the point and figure chart tan on the bar chart.

Pole   A sharp, almost vertical ascent or descent in prices, usually preceding a flag or pennant pattern (hence its name).

Price forecasting   Projecting which way a market is expected to trend. It is the crucial first step in the trading decision. The forecasting process determines whether the trader is bullish or bearish. It provides the answer to the basic question of whether to enter the market from the long or short side. If the price forecast is wrong, nothing else that follows will work.

Primary trend   A trend that usually lasts for more than a year and possibly for several years.

Pyramiding   The adding of additional positions as the market continues to move in the right direction. The actual buy or sell signal occurs on the first signal.

Random walk theory   Price changes are "serially independent" and that price history is not a reliable indicator of future price direction.

Rectangle formation   A pause in the trend during which prices move sideways between two parallel horizontal lines. The rectangle is sometimes referred to as a *trading range* or a *congestion area*. It usually represents just a consolidation period in the existing trend, and is usually resolved in the direction of the market trend that preceded its occurrence.

Relative strength index (RSI)   A ratio line comparing two different entities. It is often used to correct the erratic movement seen in constructing a momentum line because of sharp changes in the values being dropped off.

The actual formula is calculated as follows:

$$RSI = 100 - \left[\frac{100}{1 + RS} \right]$$

$$RS = \frac{\text{Average of } x \text{ day's up closes}}{\text{Average of } x \text{ days's down closes}}$$

Resistance   A price level or area *over the market* where selling pressure overcomes buying pressure and a price advance is turned back. Usually a resistance level is identified by a previous peak.

Retracement   Price action that is not in the trend's direction but that does not affect the direction of the trend itself. Generally if the action retraces more than two-thirds of the trend in progress, the movement is not temporary but rather signals a reversal. *Also known as* a correction.

Return move   A move that develops as a bounce-back to the bottom of the neckline or to the previous reaction low, both of which have now become overhead resistance. Volume may help determine the size of the bounce.

Reversal criterion   The number of boxes that the market must retrace to cause a reversal into the next column to the right. A one-box reversal means that each one-box move in either direction would be recorded. If a three-box reversal is used, then the market would have to retrace three full boxes before the next column would be started.

Reversal day   A trading day on which prices set a new extreme in the trend's direction during trading, but close in the opposite direction.

Reversal patterns   Price patterns that usually precede a reversal of the current major trend.

Runaway (measuring) gap   After the move has been underway for awhile, somewhere around the middle of the move, prices will leap forward to form a second type of gap (or a series of gaps) called the *runaway gap*. This type of gap reveals a situation where the market is moving effortlessly on moderate volume.

Saucer (bowl) pattern   A very slow and gradual change in trend from up to down or from down to up. Volume diminishes as the market makes its gradual turn, and then gradually increases as the new direction begins to take hold. The outlined pattern resembles a bowl.

Secondary (intermediate) trend   Represents corrections in the primary trend and usually lasts for three weeks to three months. These intermediate corrections usually retrace one-third to two-thirds of the previous trend. Often the retracement will be about half, or 50%.

Selling climax   After a long decline, at a major market bottom, prices suddenly drop sharply on heavy trading activity with a large decline in open interest.

Sentiment indicators   Monitor the performance of different groups such as odd lotters, mutual funds, and floor specialists. Enormous importance is place on sentiment indicators that measure the overall market bullishness and bearishness on the theory that the majority opinion is usually wrong.

Sideways pattern   A flat, horizontal price pattern.

Simple moving average   A moving average that employs an arithmetic mean. It covers the average of a ten day period and assigns equal weight to each day's price.

Spike top or bottom   This generally represents a nonpattern.

Support   A level or area on the chart *under the market* where buying interest is sufficiently strong to overcome selling pressure. Usually a support level is identified beforehand by a previous reaction low.

Symmetrical triangle (coil)   Usually a continuation pattern, it represents a pause in the existing trend after which the original trend is resumed.

Technical analysis   The study of market action, primarily through the use of charts, for the purpose of forecasting future price trends.

Technician   An analyst who bases market forecasting on price movement and other indicators.

Time filter   This technique requires that in order for a valid trend-line to be penetrated, it must be broken by a predetermined number of days, e.g., the two-day rule.

Top reversal day   A day on which a new high in an uptrend is set, followed by a lower close on the same day.

Trading range   That third of the time, by a conservative estimate, in which prices move in a flat, horizontal pattern. This type of sideways action reflects a period of equilibrium in the price level where the forces of supply and demand are in a state of relative balance.

Trend   Simply the direction of the market. Market moves are characterized by a series of zigzags. *It is the direction of those peaks and troughs that constitutes market trend.* Trends are usually classified as *major, intermediate,* or *minor.* Major trends often last for years.

Trendless   A condition in which the market is flat, having a sideways trend.

Trendline   A line drawn on a bar chart to represent a trend. In a downtrend, it is drawn down as a solid line, along successive rally peaks. In an uptrend, it is a straight line drawn along successive reaction lows.

Triangles   Usually continuation patterns, but sometimes act as reversal patterns. Although triangles are usually considered intermediate patterns, they may occasionally appear on long-term charts and take on major trend significance. The minimum requirement for a triangle is four reversal points.

Triple top or bottom   The three peaks or troughs in the *triple top or bottom* are at about the same level. The volume tends to decline with each successive peak at the top and should increase at the breakdown point. The triple top is not complete until support levels along both the intervening lows have been broken. Conversely, prices must close through the two intervening peaks at the bottom to complete a triple bottom.

Two-day reversal   A situation where, in an uptrend, prices set a new high for a move and close near the day's high. The next day, however, instead of continuing higher, prices open about unchanged and then close near the previous day's low. The opposite picture would occur at bottoms of course.

Uptrend   A series of gradually ascending peaks and troughs.

V formations or spikes   A radical departure from the tendency of markets to gradually change direction. What happens instead is an abrupt reversal of trend with little or no warning, followed by a sudden and swift move in the opposite direction. It is a nonpattern because no pattern actually exists except in hindsight.

Volume   The total amount of trading activity in that commodity market for that day. It is the total number of contracts traded during the day.

Wedge formation   A pattern that has a noticeable slant either to the upside or the downside. As a rule it slants against the prevailing trend. It is identified by two converging trendlines that come together at an *apex*. In terms of the amount of time it takes to form, the wedge usually lasts more than a month but not more than three months, putting it into the intermediate category.

Whipsaws   False signals in a trend.

X column   In a point and figure chart, represents rising prices.

Index